DEARWORTHY

Little Meditations on
the Revelations of
JULIAN of NORWICH

DEARWORTHY

Little Meditations on
the Revelations of
JULIAN of NORWICH

RUTH GORING

Copyright © Ruth Goring, 2024.

ANAMCHARA BOOKS
Vestal, New York 13850
www.AnamcharaBooks.com

All rights reserved. No part of this publication may be reproduced or transmitted for commercial purposes, except for brief quotations, without written permission of the publisher. Churches and other noncommercial interests may reproduce portions of this book without the express written permission of Anamchara Books, provided that the text does not exceed 500 words or 5 percent of the entire book, whichever is less, and that the text is not material quoted from another publisher. When reproducing text from this book, include the following credit line: "From *Dearworthy: Little Meditations on the Revelations of Julian of Norwich*, published by Anamchara Books. Used by permission."

paperback ISBN: 978-1-62524-921-0
eBook ISBN: 978-1-62524-922-7

Artwork by Ruth Goring.
Design and formatting by Micaela Grace.

Scripture quotations throughout this book are from the New Revised Standard Version Updated Edition (NRSVue). Copyright © 2021 National Council of Churches of Christ in the United States of America. Used by permission. All rights reserved worldwide.

Throughout this book, the publisher has replaced LORD with "Yahweh" wherever the original Hebrew word in scripture was YHWH, the proper name by which Divinity identified God-Self to Moses in the Book of Exodus. Because the name was considered too sacred to be spoken, YWHH or "Yahweh" was replaced with "Lord" in the Hebrew scriptures, a tradition that Christian translators continued. Bible scholars suggest the name has a range of literal meanings, including Life-Giver, Creator, the Ever-Living One, the I Am, Being, the One Who Brings into Being, the One Who Is Ever-Coming into Manifestation, and the One Who Is. Using this original sacred word is a wonderful way to move away from the patriarchal implications of "Lord." The publisher also inserted feminine pronouns into the scripture quotation on page 111.

For Claire,
held from the start
in the arms of Mother God.

CONTENTS

Invitation 9

Meditations 17

Reprise 187

Sources & Further Reading 191

Botanical Notes 199

INVITATION

All shall be well, and all shall be well, and all manner of thing shall be well.

Many years ago, this saying of Julian of Norwich fell into my heart and lodged there securely. Who wouldn't be captivated by the confidence of this voice, the beautifully rhythmic threefold repetition, with the variation "all manner of thing" serving to double-underline such a deeply comforting promise? I was a single mom, struggling financially and emotionally, and the sentence spoke to every fear I suffered: My children would be well; I would be well; we were loved and held. Time has passed, and indeed we *are* well.

My heart always leaps when Julian makes an appearance in something I am reading or in a conversation. Recently, Amy Frykholm's biography *Julian of Norwich* has taught me a great deal about Julian and her significance as the first woman to write a book in the English language (Middle English to be exact, since Julian lived from 1342 to sometime after 1416—hence the need for translators, as we can't all make sense of words like *behovely* and sentences like *Alle othere dredes sette tham emange passyons and bodelye sekeness and ymagynacions*).

We don't know very much of Julian's life before she received the series of prophetic visions she called "showings." Scholars speculate she may have been a widow and a bereaved mother: perhaps she lost her husband and child (or children) to one of the waves of bubonic plague that took many lives in Norwich, a city near England's eastern coast.

What we do know is that beginning quite early in her life, Julian desired to know God. The sacraments, daily Mass attendance, and works of service were not enough; she longed for a transformative encounter, which she expressed in a series of prayers:

- to experience Christ's Passion as if she were present at the crucifixion.

- to fall ill and come within a breath of dying.

- to survive with three "wounds": contrition, deep compassion, and longing for God.

INVITATION

The medieval spirituality expressed in these requests is quite foreign to most of us. Who wants to watch the blood and gore of a crucifixion up close, even just in the imagination? Isn't a wish for a near-death experience morbid? And don't we seek *healing* rather than *wounding*?

But we do want to know God profoundly, in our bones, our cells. Not abstractly, as a set of beliefs, but in our breath and our daily work. Even if the particulars of our wish list—the gifts we seek from God—differ from Julian's, we want *to want God more,* just as she did. The desire for God may drift away from our awareness all too often, and yet it always returns.

Julian's prayers were answered. When she was thirty and a half, she fell gravely ill, and a priest administered last rites. Some days later, as she labored desperately to breathe, her mother and caring neighbors propped her up in bed, and the parish priest returned. He set a crucifix at the foot of her bed where she could gaze at it. In her feverish state, she began to see Jesus suffering on the cross. What followed was a series of sixteen "showings" or revelations from God.

Julian spent the rest of her life with these visions, ruminating on them, asking God about them, writing them down—and twenty years later, writing them down again along with her questions and the answers God had given her, including two further showings.

Julian became not just a mystic but a theologian, recognized today as a complex and original thinker. Her writings are great gifts to all humans. Though she does not speak directly to social injustice, her visions and her implicit interactions with biblical texts invite us into the Beloved Community of restoration, equity, and love.

Will God answer our own prayers for Divine encounter, for deep nearness to Christ? Are we willing to receive wounds that might change the course of our lives?

A few years ago I started making my way through what scholars call Julian's "Long Text," the extended version that she wrote late in life. My source was *The Complete Julian of Norwich* (Paraclete, 2009), translated with extensive notes and supplemental information by Father John-Julian of the (Episcopal) Order of Julian of Norwich. Reading devotionally at bedtime, I found that one or two pages were usually enough. Again and again, I came upon sentences that took my breath away. I started writing them down and sharing them with friends.

That's where this book began. I am an artist more than a scholar, so I did not have an urge to write another biography or investigation of Julian's thought. Instead, I began to receive mental pictures of Julian's quotes that had ministered to me, set on pages decorated with leaf shapes. Those leaves have materialized here, along with other images from the plant kingdom.

Julian herself often thought in images, and they are usually "homely"—in the Middle English sense of "ordinary, familiar, day to day"—and reflect the experiences of a woman of her time. Knitting, clothing (including rags and laundry), rain dripping from eaves, and the famous single hazelnut all emerge in her effort to help readers see what she has seen.

(If Julian's hazelnut is not yet famous to you, don't worry, you'll see it later in this book.)

In the course of her long meditation on what God had shown her, Julian seems to have fallen in love with the Trinity. That threefold pattern in the "all shall be well" sentence recurs throughout the Long Text, and you will see it in some of the quotations here. She writes often of the Trinity itself, characterizing the three Persons in ways that are sometimes surprising. I hope her words bring you new joy in the triune God, as they have to me.

At some point after she received the showings, Julian became an anchorite: She moved into a tiny home attached to St. Julian's Church, where she devoted herself to prayer and contemplation. In the afternoons, townspeople would come to her porch and speak to her through a window, seeking her counsel about life and God. In that spirit, I have written some of *Dearworthy*'s meditations in the first person, an "I" voice in which I join you, dear reader, to express uncertainties, hopes, and questions about life with God. Other meditations respond with insights from Julian's work. So this little book is a dialogue.

I have chosen to focus on forty-two quotations, ranging from a single word to a short paragraph or two. Each is followed by a related text from scripture, my meditation, a question or two for you to ponder, and a breath prayer for you to try. If you grew up with lots of Bible knowledge, most of the scriptures here will be familiar to you already. I hope you'll find that setting them next to Julian's writings helps you find new depth in them, as it has for me.

For most Julian texts, I have drawn from the lovely translation by Ellyn Sanna, *All Shall Be Well* (Anamchara Books, 2018). In a few cases I quote from Fr. John-Julian's *The Complete Julian* (I've tagged these with *TCJ*).

INVITATION

Breath prayers are frequently offered in recent devotional writing, but this way of praying is many centuries old. The classic Christian breath prayer, known as the Jesus Prayer, is (inhale) "Lord Jesus Christ, Son of God," (exhale) "have mercy on me, a sinner." The practice involves becoming conscious of breath and using it to maintain a rhythm of repetitive prayer.

Repetition in itself adds no force to our prayers, as Jesus reminded us in his Sermon on the Mount (Matthew 6:7–8)—but repeated breath prayers can help us bring peace and faith into our bodies. As these very short prayers join the rhythm of our breath, they remind us of what is true and help us (our lungs, abdomen, the very pores in our skin) believe it.

Years ago, I learned to count seconds for deep breathing: four seconds for the inhale (one-one hundred, two-one hundred, three-one hundred, four-one hundred) and eight for the exhale. That's why the exhale portion of the breath prayers I've included in this book is often longer. Sometimes, though, it felt right to exhale just a brief phrase. Stretch out the words as they flow through you, and let your lungs empty fully.

Quite early in these meditations, I introduce "Mother God" as a way to address God and to talk about God. Julian, in her original writing, uses male pronouns in reference to

God (as was customary in her day), yet she spends quite a bit of time on God's mothering—specifically on Jesus as the very source and exemplar of what mothering is. She's not by any means the only mystic to have this insight, but she develops it so convincingly that my language of prayer has changed in response.

At the end of the book, you'll find notes to various meditations where I quote or draw on the work of a particular writer, along with some reading recommendations. After that, I've included a botanical list keyed to the number of the meditation with which each illustration is paired. I provide common and species names, native region, and often a snippet of personal experience or feeling about these plants. Drawing them led me into what I can only call a kind of interspecies intimacy as I looked so deeply at each petal, spike, and vein.

Julian's brilliant writings have shocked me into joy again and again. May they also fill you with wonder and deepen your faith.

MEDITATIONS

a deep longing to be wounded . . .
to have a firm and unfailing desire
for God's presence

1

How long, O Yahweh?
Will you forget me forever?
How long will you hide your face from me?

PSALM 13:1

Is God hiding from me, or am I hiding *my* face from God? It's quite possible I'm the one hiding because I don't want to be wounded. I'm not sure I can trust God.

Or maybe I'm just wired wrong. Other people are emotionally open and able to sense God's presence, but I don't have that talent.

Maybe God is the one hiding, out of displeasure with me. I have failed to be generous or honest or hardworking. I have deceived myself and others. Do I deserve blame, God's face averted?

But I do want to know God better and to enjoy God's love. Something in me reaches toward that Presence. I suspect that more beauty and love exists than I've known thus far. Surely there is a greater freedom than I've known thus far.

A longing as a wound—it seems so strange that Julian prayed for contrition, compassion, and longing for God *as wounds*. Masochistic maybe. I don't want more pain. I've had enough to last a lifetime.

I already have wounds.

Questions

Could my wounds become openings for God?

Will God be gentle with me?

Breath Prayer

inhale: Please earn my trust.

exhale: Here is my small desire.

dearworthy

2

I have loved you with an everlasting love.

JEREMIAH 31:3

Dearworthy became one of my favorite words after I encountered it in Julian. It means "loved, prized, honored," and she first applies it to Jesus's precious blood, then to his mother Mary. At first, I thought Julian had coined the word, but it turns out to be a common term in use in her day. Still, it's so frequent in her writing and so characteristic of her understanding of the relationship between God and human beings that I chose it as this book's title.

After describing her vision of Christ's Passion—his suffering on the cross—and exploring its meaning, Julian begins applying *dearworthy* as God's own term of endearment for all of us. She says that despite Jesus's exalted place at God's side, he remains ever "friendly" and "homely" toward us and seeks to raise us up and honor us. At a time when the established church in England taught that dying with unconfessed sin could mean eternal torment in hell, Julian became deeply convinced that God looks on us not with anger and blame but with love and friendliness.

I shared my discovery of *dearworthy* in Julian's writings with a good friend who is nonreligious because she has not (yet) been able to access a sense of God's love. We call each other *Dearworthy* now. She is a likeable, ethically sensitive person who gives her life to serving others—but even if she were difficult to like, God would see her as dear, worthy of great love.

Before anything, after everything, and in this very moment, *you* are dearworthy.

MEDITATIONS

Questions

Do I experience Jesus as my dearworthy friend?

Why or why not?

Breath Prayer

inhale (receiving from God): You are dearworthy.

exhale (responding to God): You are dearworthy.

The Trinity is our Maker.
The Trinity is our Keeper.
The Trinity is our everlasting Lover.

3

The grace of the Lord Jesus Christ,
the love of God,
and the communion of the Holy Spirit
be with all of you.

2 CORINTHIANS 13:13

Wound, *dearworthy*, *Trinity*: These are some of Julian's favorite words.

The Divine Three-in-Oneness is Julian's ocean. She dives deep into it again and again, then surfaces joyfully, calling out new names for the Three. She revels in the Trinity's richness—the multiplicity and absolute unity within the Godhead. In naming the Divine Persons, she follows Hagar, the first human in the Jewish Bible to choose a name for God: *El-roi* in Hebrew, translated as "the God of seeing" or "the God who sees" (Genesis 16:13).

Julian's names, too, often arise from what God does and how the Three Persons relate to us. God the Creator makes us, Jesus keeps us, the Holy Spirit loves us.

Have you ever thought of the Holy Spirit as Lover? I confess that though I have felt the Spirit's presence many times, my mental picture has been of a conduit or channel of Divine love and wisdom, rather than of the Spirit herself as a source of love. Julian, however, sees more clearly: Despite her delight in naming the role of each Divine Person, she says repeatedly that anything done by one Person is actually done by all Three; for example, she says that "wherever Jesus is, the Trinity is there as well" (chap. 4). Amy Frykholm, the author of the biography I read about Julian, says that in Julian's understanding, "God is fundamentally and inextricably a relation of love. When you perceive any one person of the Trinity, you experience them all—if you have perceived the presence of love."

The Trinity is a mystery. Not like a murder mystery, a puzzle to be unlocked so we know whom to blame. Instead, the mysteries of God are great lands for us to journey into, oceans for us to swim in. The Trinity is love, delight, and mutual gaze.

Question

What are some of your own favorite names for the Members of the Trinity?

Breath Prayer

inhale: You make me, you keep me.

exhale: Show me how you love me.

The happy comfort revealed to me
is big enough for us all.

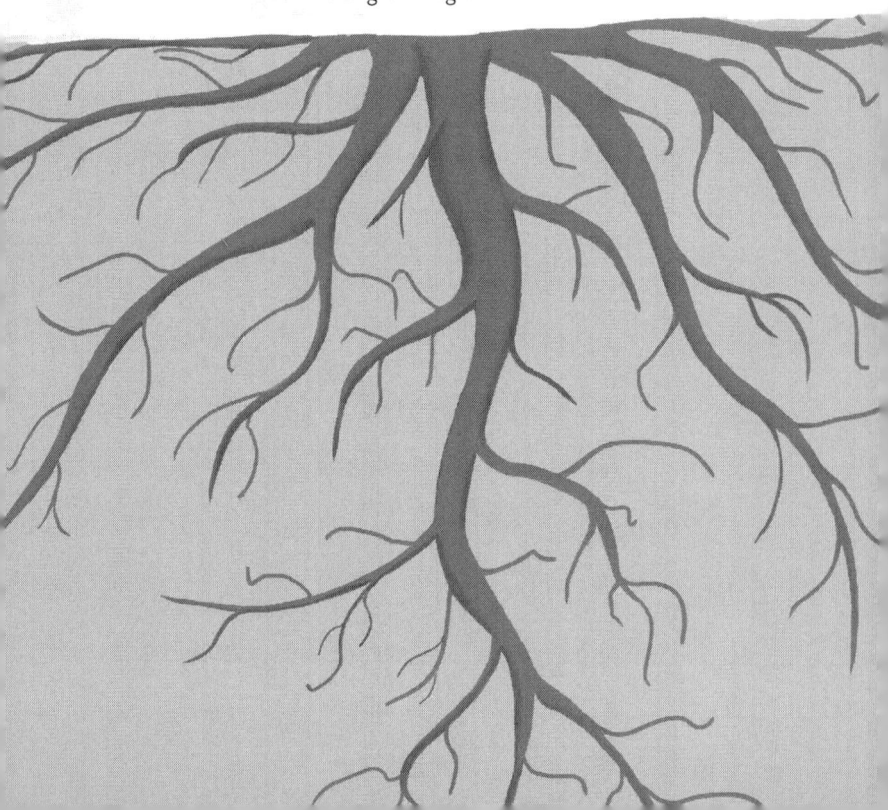

4

*For as all die in Adam,
so all will be made alive in Christ.*

1 CORINTHIANS 15:22

Julian's promise of God's "happy comfort" comes near the end of her writing, but you get to read this sentence early in this series of meditations because it's a very inviting use of another of Julian's favorite words: *all*. You will encounter it again later: All will be well, God's love is for all, God's goodness is for all, drawing us all into awareness of our belonging to each other.

Have you ever noticed that *all* is one of the apostle Paul's favorite words as well? The 1 Corinthians verse that begins this meditation is only one instance. I find that at different times in my life, I notice different things. For instance, I have read Luke and Acts, noting every mention of women; at other times, I have read these books noticing every mention of the poor or every mention of the Holy Spirit. Recently, I've been astonished by the frequency of words like *all* and *everyone* in Paul's letters.

All, *everyone*, and *the world* (the entire cosmos) occur at significant points in John's Gospel too. In John 12:32, Jesus says, "When I am lifted up, I will draw *all people* to myself." The Good News of Jesus focuses on *inclusion*.

Many of us, however, grew up in a version of Christianity focused on exclusion: the belief that human beings who reject God—or who had no opportunity to know about the true God—will burn in hell forever. If you still hold to that teaching, you may feel uneasy when you read Julian's repeated assertions that God loves *all* and is rescuing *all of us*. But she is simply echoing a word Jesus used, that the apostle Paul used.

Dwell in the word *all*, taste its vastness, turn it over in your mouth. It is one of Jesus's own words.

Questions

How do you feel about the word all
in Julian's writing and in the Christian scriptures?

Try substituting some *for* all *in the scriptures quoted above.
How would that change their meaning?*

Breath Prayer

inhale: Your comfort is enough for all.

exhale: Help me believe and rest.

Those of us who are under heaven
come there by means of our longing and desire.
(Longing is the road we travel,
and desire is our road map.)

5

My God, my God, why have you forsaken me?
Why are you so far from helping me,
from the words of my groaning?

PSALM 22:1

Julian's Long Text begins with a quick summary of the showings she received, then backtracks to explain the desires that preceded them. For example, "I thought I already had some feeling for Christ's endurance [in his suffering on the cross], but I longed for more" (chap. 2). She goes on to articulate the other desires that had crystallized in her devotional life (which I summarized in my introduction to these meditations).

Writers today often evaluate short stories and novels in terms of "what's at stake." Every good story starts with an unmet need, an unfulfilled desire. The story leads us along with the protagonist in their quest to satisfy their desire—and sometimes to purify it. If the character's desire or need is too muddy or simply trivial, most readers will lose interest. We want stories where the struggles are worthwhile, where the outcome matters.

Julian begins her story with her desire for nearness to God. And because we too need God, we keep reading to see whether and how her desires are fulfilled. The stakes are not "heaven versus hell" as our eternal destiny; she mentions no fear of condemnation to unending torment. But they are very high stakes: As she receives revelations and asks God about them, she wrestles with the problem of evil. How can an ineffably good and powerful God tolerate a creation in which God's creatures suffer so much harm?

The answers she receives reassure her deeply, though she needs to hear them more than once. And so she leads us on the road of longing, letting her desire for God's love and goodness map the way.

If we felt no need for more of God, we would never embark on a path of prayer, sacred reading, and other spiritual disciplines. Our need opens us up, our longing forges a path, and our desire deepens as we begin to encounter God. Or perhaps we mostly encounter silence and must be patient and persevering. Julian will help us with both the seeking and the finding.

MEDITATIONS

Questions

*What profound need
are you aware of at this stage of your life?*

Have you ever spoken or written your desire to God?

Breath Prayer

inhale: I need you.

exhale: Increase my desire.

In my confusion, I always wondered why
God's great and wise foreknowledge
had not prevented evil.
If God had, I thought,
all would have been well.

6

The people will be oppressed,
everyone by another
and everyone by a neighbor;
the youth will be insolent to the elder
and the base to the honorable.

ISAIAH 3:5

Julian uses the word *well* frequently to express her desire for the world, so I looked up the etymology. *Well* in her day was understood to mean abundant, as desired, satisfying, lacking nothing. Julian was essentially seeking the Hebrew state of *shalom*: peace, well-being, healthy relationships, love.

How can things become well, Julian asks, when evil seems to permeate the world so thoroughly? Wouldn't all have been well if sin had been prevented in the first place? Couldn't God have thrown up an impenetrable barrier against it?

Then we would have perfection and symmetry, free of blemishes or suffering. Julian longed for such innocence and worried hard over God's reasons for allowing sin. "I ought much to have given up this disturbing wondering," she admits ruefully, "but nevertheless, I made mourning and sorrow about it without reason or discretion" (*TCJ,* chap. 27).

I'm glad the questions troubled her. They trouble me too. I will never forget one night in my young adulthood when having learned of a baby born with a genetic abnormality that caused chronic pain, I tossed, turned, and wept in bed. The child was receiving tender care at my parents' foster home, but still, how could a good God have allowed this? How could God ever make it up to this little child?

You may well have endured a night like that. Or a day, or a week, or many months. You may *be* that child, suffering incurable chronic pain.

How can all be well?

MEDITATIONS

Question

Why?

Breath Prayer

inhale: It's too much of too much.

exhale: I want to be whole.

But Jesus—who was showing me
all that I needed to know—
answered these thoughts now
and said,
"Sin was unavoidable.
But all shall be well,
and all shall be well,
and absolutely everything
shall be well."

7

*We know that all things work together
for good for those who love God,
who are called according to his purpose.*

ROMANS 8:28

In Julian's Middle English, Jesus tells her that sin is "behovely." There's some discussion among translators about this word's meaning. The phrase "it behooves us to" incorporates a more recent version of the term: we need to do *x*; it is the right thing to do. *Behovely* could mean necessary. It could also mean appropriate. Ellyn Sanna's translation is *unavoidable*, and similarly, the late Father John-Julian chose *inevitable*.

Jesus doesn't answer Julian's how-question directly, but he seems to be saying that sin (which has no being in itself but is parasitic on God's good Creation) becomes an occasion for something beautiful. Because of Adam and Eve's fall, the Second Person of the Trinity fell into Creation and identified with its suffering, becoming the Child of Humanity. The story of God's involvement with the world is still being told. It is a story of redemption, of movement toward shalom.

Jesus the Protector doesn't say *shalom*, of course; he uses Julian's own word, *well*. It's sweet that Divinity offers Julian this mirroring, the way a human mother repeats her toddler's words to affirm them and maybe help the child to pronounce them more clearly.

Julian has rebuked herself for her desperate struggle, but Mother God does not scold her. Quite the opposite.

Your desire is good, Mother God says. *It is my very purpose.* The promise is never conditional: Indeed all *shall* be well—abundant, lacking nothing, satisfying.

Question

Will God's promise hold me?

Breath Prayer

inhale: All shall be well.

exhale: Every single thing shall be well.

The Spirit showed me a tiny thing
the size of a hazelnut, as round as a ball
and so small I could hold it
in the palm of my hand.
I looked at it in my mind's eye
and wondered, "What is this?"
The answer came to me:
"This is everything that has been made.
This is all Creation."

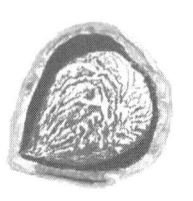

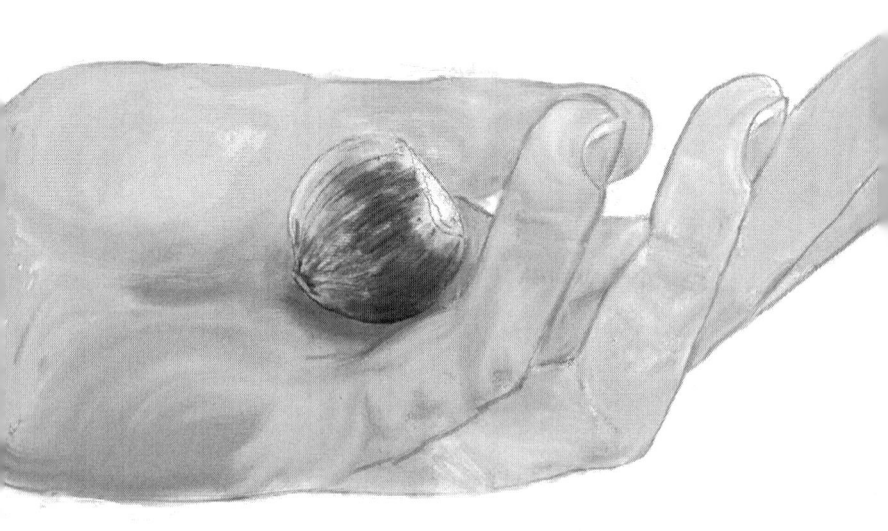

8

In [God's] hand are the depths of the earth;
the heights of the mountains are his also.
The sea is his, for he made it,
and the dry land, which his hands have formed.

PSALM 95:4–5

It's not really a nut that Julian sees; it is a round object the *size* of a hazelnut. It is alive but so very small and vulnerable. And it represents all of Creation.

Whether Julian is thinking of only the Earth or a whole cosmos, she predates Copernicus and Galileo with their insights into Earth as a round planet orbiting the Sun. She does not, however, envision Earth as floating in a vast universe of galaxies, just one of the countless orbiting spheres they contain. Instead, "all that is made" reveals itself to her as round; not fastened in place, only held.

The lyricist who wrote Psalm 95 is marveling at God's greatness in creating and holding the whole Earth; the focus is on the power of the Divine hands. The marvel for Julian comes from the opposite direction: What she sees is the smallness of creation relative to her own hand. Both images are arresting, but they serve different purposes.

Over and over again, Julian sees God and the world as a mother sees. The universe is fragile and needs gentle care. The Protector must watch it carefully and treat it with Divine kindness.

Questions

How have you become aware recently of Earth's fragility?

What in your own life feels especially fragile and at risk?

Breath Prayer

inhale: Hold us in tenderness.

exhale: Grant us your peace.

It was so small that I marveled it could endure.
Such a tiny thing seemed likely
to simply fall into nothingness.
Again the answer came to my thoughts:
"It lasts, and it wll always last,
because God loves it."
Everything—all that exists—
draws its being from God's love."

9

The whole creation has been groaning together
as it suffers together the pains of labor,
and not only the creation, but we ourselves,
who have the first fruits of the Spirit,
groan inwardly while we wait for adoption,
the redemption of our bodies.
For in hope we were saved.

ROMANS 8:22–24

Julian marvels at the vulnerability of Creation. How does this place, this reality, this Creation, not come apart and fall into oblivion? What holds it together?

Nowadays, our questions are much the same as we face climate change and the challenging political choices required to slow its progression. How does our fragile Earth hold together and maintain climates that are friendly to life? Will God somehow reverse the damage that humans have done?

What of *this* favorite place—your own special spot on the planet, with its water and air and trees? Will it survive?

As usual in Julian's conversations with God, her how-question doesn't get a direct answer, and I'm sure ours won't either, at least not in the moment. But she is given a resounding affirmation and a why: *It continues and always shall, because God loves it.*

God loves it is the reason for anything to continue in existence. Mother God's love is the sturdiest force there is.

We can't deny that species are going extinct, and that some places seem altered beyond repair by industrial farming, overfishing, or rising temperatures. But because God loves the whole Creation and always will, we can hope, keep our eyes open for promising signs, and do our bit to participate in Mother God's repairing work.

MEDITATIONS

Questions

Where do you see signs of Earth's wounding?

Where do you see hopeful changes?

Breath Prayer

inhale: Mother of all life . . .

exhale: We hope in your love.

Some deeds appear so evil from our perspective,
so hurtful and damaging,
that no good could possibly come from them.

10

I see violence and strife in the city . . .

ruin is in its midst.

PSALM 55:9, 11

Julian's confidence that "absolutely everything shall be well" does not come easily. She writes of asking God some version of this question more than once: *How* can all be well given the seeming intractability of evil in our world?

Intractable: stuck; impossible to resolve.

Remember that Julian lived through more than one epidemic of bubonic plague in her hometown. She lived in a time of political turbulence as well: In 1381, the Peasants' Revolt spread east- and northward across England, as peasants, artisans, and even some village officials protested in the streets and set fire to public buildings, calling for lower taxes and an end to the landowner-serf system. The revolt reached

Norwich quickly, where many "common" people of the town joined it. Meanwhile, the bishop of Norwich pulled together an armed band to fight on the side of the king. In the end, more than fifteen hundred rebels were killed, and the king's promise to end serfdom was rescinded.

Intractable: war, the bombing of civilians, genocide. Climate change as corporations and governments insist on quick money from the extraction and burning of fossil fuels. Abuse we have suffered; the abuse of children. Spiritual words that trap us instead of freeing us.

Whether it's personal suffering or evil being done in our name in some other land, there is pain we can't fix. And sometimes God seems utterly silent.

Today carry the questions and the prayer in your breath and body as you walk. If you are not able to walk, hum them as you go through the day. Let them flow through you.

Questions

Is there pain God is asking me to carry?

Is there pain I am to let go?

Breath Prayer

inhale: Keep me from despair.

exhale: Strengthen me in hope.

The only answer I received was this:
"That which is impossible to you
is not impossible for me.

I will keep my word in all things,
and I will make absolutely everything well.

11

"For nothing will be impossible with God."

Luke 1:37 (the angel Gabriel)

Jesus said to his disciples,
"Truly I tell you, it will be hard
for a rich person to enter the kingdom of heaven.
Again I tell you, it is easier for a camel
to go through the eye of a needle
than for someone who is rich
to enter the kingdom of God."
When the disciples heard this,
they were greatly astounded and said,
"Then who can be saved?"
But Jesus looked at them and said,
"For mortals it is impossible,
but for God all things are possible."

Matthew 19:23–26

What God is doing in the world is passing strange. Julian is surprised again and again by what is revealed to her in the showings, just as in Luke, Elizabeth is surprised to conceive John in her old age, and then Mary is startled by Gabriel's announcement that she will give birth to the Coming One. Likewise in Matthew, Jesus's disciples are repeatedly perplexed by his teachings and actions. God comes to us with impossibilities!

The Julian quotation on page 58 is God's answer to her deep anxiety in the previous meditation: Some evil seems too great to be undone and redeemed, even by God. Notice that God again does not explain *how* this upending of evil will happen. The Holy One simply says, *I will make absolutely everything well.* The promise is given—a huge promise, a handle for Julian and for us to grasp when despair is near.

Isn't it interesting that Jesus's assertion of Divine possibilities follows his statement that rich people cannot enter God's Beloved Community? Maybe needle eyes were larger in his day, but it was still absurd to imagine that a camel could squeeze through one. Think about the enormity of economic inequality in our day. For example, toward the end of 2023, "66.6 percent of the total wealth in the United States was owned by the top 10 percent of earners. In comparison, the lowest 50 percent of earners only owned 2.6

percent of the total wealth" (according to Statista, a company that aggregates data and research). Those percentages represent injustice; they involve real human beings who struggle to save anything, who are one paycheck away from disaster. Can such inequality ever be undone?

Jesus says that bringing rich people into God's family is not impossible with God. That's because Jesus's way is to bring down the wealthy and powerful while raising up the poor and lowly. Once there is equality, the needle's eye will be a spacious door, easy for us all to walk through.

Another world is possible with God.

Questions

What impossibilities are you facing, in the world or in your life?

Can you imagine God upending these hardships or evils?

Breath Prayer

inhale: For God all things are possible.

exhale: Nothing will be impossible for God.

"Look and see!
I will use the same strength,
wisdom, and goodness
I used to accomplish humanity's
safety and wholeness

to make well
all that is not well
—and you will see it!"

12

The creation waits with eager longing
for the revealing of the children of God,
. . . in hope that the creation itself will be set free
from its enslavement to decay
and will obtain the freedom
of the glory of the children of God.

ROMANS 8:19–21

Paul's words in Romans express the longing we feel on behalf of the Earth, and Julian's Protector voices the same promise he's given again and again: All longings for fulfillment and healing—even those of the nonhuman Creation—will be satisfied.

God also speaks to Julian in the Trinitarian terms that are becoming familiar to us at this point in our relationship with her. The attributes the Divine will use to make all things well are also Julian's names for the Persons of the Trinity. To heal the world, God will pull out all the stops, acting as Strength, Wisdom, and Goodness, the Three-in-One whose purpose is always love.

Do you have courage to receive this joy? To look squarely at evil and suffering takes a courage we don't always have. Accepting joy, in a world filled with prejudice, division, and violence, takes courage too. Often, I would much rather immerse myself in a good murder mystery—an imagined problem that I can try to solve in my imagination—than listen to news of the latest violence in my city or on the other side of the world. Murder mysteries are fine, of course—as long as I'm not closing myself off long-term to the needs of others. God calls me (and you) to be co-workers with the Divine work of shalom.

The strength, wisdom, and goodness of God are dedicated, right now, right here, and in all other times and places, to finishing the job of making us well, healing every wrong, overturning every injustice, setting Creation free to flourish. Sometimes, we catch glimpses of this work. Sometimes, we get to take part in it.

Four Quartets, T. S. Eliot's masterpiece, includes the line: "Humankind cannot bear very much reality." Eliot may have meant the burden of daily tedium, but I think he also was thinking of the challenge of holding great pain or great joy. We are limited, and we need not feel guilty about that. But empathy deepens us, and so do the moments when our hearts lift in hope and wonder.

Questions

Does hoping for personal or social restoration scare you?

What moments of great joy have you experienced?

Breath Prayer

inhale: Your power is love.

exhale: Your wisdom and goodness are only love.

After this our good Protector said to me,
"Thank you for your hard work.
Thank you especially for giving me your youth."

13

[The landowner who paid
all his hired men equally says:]
"I choose to give to this last the same as I give to you.
Am I not allowed to do what I choose
with what belongs to me?
Or are you envious because I am generous?"
[Jesus concludes:] "So the last will be first,
and the first will be last."

MATTHEW 20:14–16

What Julian hears from God is hard to grasp. The scriptures—especially Psalms, Paul's letters, and Jesus's teachings and example—are full of calls to praise and thank God. But God thanking us? I can't recall any scriptures to back this up explicitly, nor have I seen God's gratitude as a subject in any of the theological books I've read over the years. Who would expect *God's* thanks for the small services we're able to render?

But Julian hears God thanking her. The mutuality she experiences with God shocks her again and again. Later in the same chapter, she returns to this insight. Those who commit themselves early to participating in God's work enjoy special rewards: God's gratitude, all Creation's awareness of it, and eternal awe and joy in this gratitude.

She wrote:

> I saw that each person's age shall be made known in heaven with a sweet intimacy and familiarity, thus honoring each one for how she used the time she was given. Those who willingly and freely offered their youth to God are thanked with special reverence.
>
> But it did not matter how long a man or woman had turned toward God on Earth, whether for an instant, a day, or an entire lifetime. In the end, each person experiences all three levels of joy.

Anything at all we have done, however fleeting, to love and serve God prompts Divinity's full gratitude (paralleling the landowner's full payment of all the workers in Jesus's parable in Matthew 20). God's generosity to us exceeds programs like affirmative action and even reparations, since these are just minimal efforts to acknowledge both the violence Black and Indigenous people have suffered and the uncompensated contributions they and their ancestors have made to our society. Perhaps the envy of the earliest workers hired in the parable is similar to the way I (and white Americans like me) tend to cling to privilege.

There are no spiritual elites. God's glory is for us all.

Questions

*How do you feel about this idea,
that God gives thanks to human beings?*

*Listen to the Spirit:
What might God be thanking you for?*

Breath Prayer

inhale God's thanks: Dearworthy, I thank you.

exhale your gratitude: I thank you, Mother God.

I saw Christ as a homeowner
who has called all his beloved servants
and friends to a formal dinner, a stately celebration.
I realized our Protector did not
take his place at the table.
Instead, he was present everywhere,
making sure all his guests were always comfortable
and enjoying themselves.

He treated his guests with such courtesy and welcome,
singing them a song of endless love.

14

The kingdom of heaven may be compared to a king who gave a wedding banquet for his son.

MATTHEW 22:2

Julian would have been familiar with Jesus's banquet parables (which you can find mostly in Matthew 22 and 25 and Luke 14) via sermons and possibly medieval mystery plays. Perhaps the "supper of the Lamb" (in Revelation 19:6–9) shaped her vision as well. She draws on Jesus's original imagery and emphasizes the host's generosity.

First, Jesus as a wealthy householder throws a party, and everyone is invited. But it's far from the kind of banquet a medieval British lord would have hosted. This host, instead of sitting in an elegant chair and receiving homage from his guests, walks around mingling with everyone there. He pauses to speak with each of them, to ask if they are comfortable and having a good time, and he is gratified when they say yes.

The servants in this story are not hovering to offer food and meet the guests' needs. The servants are guests. *The host is the only active servant.*

Julian's vision may remind you of Jesus's shocking service to his followers when he washed their dusty feet (John 13). We can also recall these words he spoke to his friends: "I do not call you servants any longer, because the servant does not know what the master is doing, but I have called you friends, because I have made known to you everything that I have heard from my Father" (John 15:15–16). Servants and friends are indistinguishable from each other at the Divine banquet; there is no class division.

And the Host has not hired professional performers to entertain his guests. Instead, he provides the music himself, singing a song of endless love.

Questions

*Think of Jesus as your host, welcoming you.
What feelings arise?*

What might it mean to be God's guest in Creation?

Breath Prayer

inhale: Let me hear your song.

exhale: Teach me to sing with you.

Christ not only pays attention
to high and great things,
things that are obvious and important,
but also, equally,
to small things
that seem trivial,
simple, and hidden. . . .
Not even the least thing
will be forgotten.

15

Are not five sparrows sold for two pennies?
Yet not one of them is forgotten in God's sight.
But even the hairs of your head are all numbered.

LUKE 12:6–7

Through [Christ] God was pleased to reconcile
to himself all things,
whether on earth or in heaven.

COLOSSIANS 1:20

An endangered beetle—*Rhadine infernalis*—lives only in Bexar, a county in Texas. Seldom seen because it inhabits karsts—caves too small for humans to enter—it abides in permanent low light. It has evolved to have a long life (for a beetle), while at the same time, needing little food.

Nevertheless, human development has endangered it: The entrances to the small caves where it lives are being capped, cutting off its water supply. Destruction of the surrounding ecosystems is another aspect of the danger humans have caused this creature.

You can check out photos of *R. infernalis* online. Trust me, you wouldn't want to see it in your kitchen. But Jesus, Julian, and Paul all tell us that God cares for it. Somehow, it too will be part of the restoration of all things, the new creation.

Small creatures, small tasks: none are dismissed by God. Not the common violets and dandelions in my yard (considered weeds by some people). Not the piping plovers that nest on a busy Chicago beach. Not my neighbor's vegetable garden or an artist's painstaking effort to capture light on glossy skin or the exact shape of a leaf. And not a child's distress over their math homework either. God cares for them all.

Of course, we humans do not have infinite attention and energy; we must prioritize, discern what's ours to love and care for. But we can do so knowing that God created, loves, and redeems *all things*. The breathtaking assertion of Colossians 1, which Julian so beautifully echoes, is that Jesus's endurance and victory on the cross is for *all*. Nothing and no one is left out or forgotten. Nothing is too small.

Questions

What have you assumed is too small for God to care about?

How do you feel about these expansive promises?

Breath Prayer

inhale: Nothing is forgotten.

exhale: You hold all in love.

We began to exist
when God created us—
and divine love for us
has no beginning.
Our beginnnings sprang
from that love.

16

As the Father has loved me,
so I have loved you;
abide in my love.

JOHN 15:9

Eastern Orthodox theology teaches that the cosmos, including Earth and us human beings, was created from the overflow of the eternal love within the triune God. When I first came upon this teaching, chills ran down my spine.

This understanding of the "social Trinity"—the love that flows eternally among the divine Persons—took me back instantly to the memory of a moment in my early childhood when I happened to look up and see my parents exchange a loving touch and glance. I was flooded with a sense of deep security. Looking back, I realize I needed to know my parents loved me, but just as much, I needed to be sure *they loved each other.* Their love anchored me in the world. Their love for each other surrounded and fortified their love for my siblings and me.

Even if your human parents weren't able to give you the gift of their mutual love, your beginning and your life day to day are rooted forever in the Trinity's love. Look up and see their gaze of mutual delight.

Questions

*What does it mean for the universe
to be formed from love's overflow?*

*Have you experienced more-than-enough,
plenty-to-share human love?*

And if not, do you still bear wounds from this lack?

Breath Prayer

inhale: Love everlasting . . .

exhale: You make me and hold me.

Our kind Protector
does not want us to despair,
no matter how often or badly we fall,
for our failures do not get in the way
of Divine love.

17

*Just as one man's [Adam's] trespass
led to condemnation for all,
so one man's [Jesus's] act of righteousness
leads to justification and life for all.*

Romans 5:18

"Sin has no substance, no being," says Julian. If sin had existence in itself, it would have been created by God. Since there is no evil in God, it's impossible for sin to *be*: "It can only be known through the pain it causes," says Julian (chap. 27).

Julian considers sin a violation of our innate nature, which is to love God. In one of the showings, she sees a lord seated in dignity with a servant nearby. The lord asks the servant to take care of a certain task, and the young man leaps up to obey—but immediately stumbles and falls. Instead of berating the servant for his awkwardness, the lord descends from the throne and kindly takes his hand to help him up. He sees the good intentions of the bumbling young man, and it pleases him greatly.

Continuing to reflect on this little parable/revelation, Julian echoes Paul's patterning of Adam and Christ in Romans 5: Adam fell into sin and death, but God took on flesh and "fell" into human life in order to raise us all up into the life of the Trinity—what we were made for all along. Julian also hears Jesus on the cross say he was *glad* to suffer with and for us, that we are worth his pain.

She concludes that sin does not preoccupy God, because the remedy already has been provided. In the latter part of the Long Text, she writes about sin again, wanting to make sure, I think, that no one assumes that it's fine to sin deliberately. Obviously, harming ourselves and other people is destructive. Our joy comes from adoring God and honoring the Divine nature in ourselves and in each other.

Paul opens Romans 6 with the rhetorical question "Should we continue in sin in order that grace may increase?" (v. 1). Of course not! He goes on to say, if we have been made alive in Christ, why in the world would we want to return to death?

Still, in the small and large "falls" of our lives, God is ever ready to lift us up. And the Holy One never reproaches us with an *I-told-you-so*.

Questions

Is there a blaming voice in your head?

What does Psalm 103:10–14 say to your heart?

Breath Prayer

inhale: What I really want is you.

exhale: Let me always face the light.

God wants to be known.
The Divine One is pleased when we rest
in the Spirit's presence,
since all that was created will
never be enough in and of itself
to give us what we need.

18

*Take delight in Yahweh,
and God will give you the desires of your heart.*

PSALM 37:4

Mutual desire: Normally we apply that phrase to romantic and erotic love between two human beings. We don't think of mutual desire between God and ourselves.

For a good part of my life, I assumed God loves us unconditionally with parental benevolence, but it never occurred to me that God *needs* us. We try to return God's love because it's good for us and Christians *should* love God out of gratitude for our salvation. It's challenging, though, because Divinity is often opaque to us, hard to find.

But Julian says *God wants to be known.* That changes things. God's love for us includes a desire to be near, to be known, seen, heard. The Divine desires us far more than we desire Divinity. We go through times of feeling distant—what the mystics call dark nights of the soul—but not because God has withdrawn from us. We merely have more growing to do.

Father Thomas Green proposes that in our darkest "nights," our struggle to see God may have to do with God's nearness rather than absence. Think of being cheek to cheek in the dark with someone you love. You can't see them clearly up so close—their features are dim and fuzzy—but that's just a side effect of intimacy.

We are still learning how to be intimate with God. Sometimes we get disoriented, and we don't realize God is holding us gently close.

What about our other desires, for safety, the meeting of physical needs, human companionship, good work, a sense of purpose, flourishing communities? Both the psalmist and Julian seem to be saying that these are healthy—but by themselves, they are too small.

As we learn to live face-to-face with God, we expand and become more fully ourselves. We begin to make out God's features more clearly. We long for justice and healing in the world and in ourselves, and God's gaze of love and desire strengthens us with hope.

MEDITATIONS

Questions

*Have you ever experienced
a yearning you knew at a deep level?*

*What do you feel when you think
of God's desire to be known?*

Breath Prayer

inhale: Your desire honors me.

exhale: Whom do I have in heaven but you?

And that is why we may humbly ask
our Divine Lover for whatever we want.
For our natural and innate desire is for God—
and God's desire is for us.

19

Is there anyone among you who,
if your child asked for bread, would give a stone?
or if the child asked for a fish, would give a snake?
If you, then, who are evil,
know how to give good gifts to your children,
how much more will your Father in heaven
give good things to those who ask him!

MATTHEW 7:9–11

Whatever we want, says Julian. *How much more,* says Jesus. Want, pray, ask: That's a very complex and layered set of verbs.

A lot of us who grew up in conservative Christian spaces learned that our wishes and desires were always suspect. We were taught that what God wanted for us would generally turn out to be something we didn't want. Thankfully, many of us have unlearned that ingrained suspicion. We've learned that when we ignore our intuitions and deep desires, we run into trouble.

Still, our consumer culture is built on stirring up wants and wishes that are far more shallow in nature. "You *deserve* this," say the kind, authoritative voices in commercials. And maybe we do. Nevertheless, marketers and the corporations that pay them can't be trusted to help us figure out who we are and what will help us thrive.

And of course, God does *not* give us everything we pray for. We may think we want something that would actually make us unhappy and unhealthy. We may experience a particular yearning we would never turn into a prayer request because we know its satisfaction would harm others.

And through all this, God simply draws prayer from us. The Life Giver wants to hear about our desires and how we process them. The Divine is not a magician solving all our problems but a Parent who leans toward us as we work through our struggles, offering us the rich gifts we need: bread, not stones; fish, not snakes.

Julian says that our natural desire is *to have God*. At times, that longing is not really present in our awareness. But our Parent understands. The Divine knows that growing up is very hard, that being human involves many needs, and at any given moment some needs obscure others.

Let's go ahead; let's bring to God all that we wish. Let's see if Jesus's *how much more* promise bears out.

Questions

Do you trust your desires?

Try digging under specific desires to find if deeper ones lie beneath. What does this reveal?

Breath Prayer

inhale: All that we wish and ask . . .

exhale: How much more you give.

The Fiend is overcome
by Christ's love and endurance.

20

Since, therefore, [God's] children
share flesh and blood,
[Christ] himself likewise shared the same things,
so that through death he might destroy
the one who has the power of death,
that is, the devil, and free those who all their lives
were held in slavery by the fear of death.

HEBREWS 2:14–15

*D*evil, Satan, Enemy, Accuser, fiend: Scripture and church tradition give us multiple names for the evil that invaded God's good creation. In the days of Julian's great illness, in the midst of the Divine showings, demonic apparitions also challenged her spiritually. But then she saw them dispersed by Jesus's suffering on the cross.

While Julian takes evil seriously, her writing does not reflect the fear of the devil and hell that we often hear in certain church sermons. The homilies of her time and place also frequently appealed to this fear, but any anxiety she may have harbored has lost its hold in the light of God's powerful love. She says,

> No matter how much [the Fiend] labors, he continually sees souls escape his grasp by virtue of Christ's Endurance. This is his misery, for although God allows him to work in our world, each of his actions is turned to joy by Divine action. He might as well not do anything at all, for his efforts come to nothing. All his strength is absorbed by God and turned to good. (chap. 13)

As for hell itself, Julian asks God for a glimpse, but she sees exactly nothing. "The revelations I received," she muses, "focused only on goodness, with little mention of evil" (chap. 13). And so she, like the author of Hebrews, returns to marveling at Christ's "fall" into the human condition, his full experience of death that silences the Accuser, liberates human beings from death's horror, and begins the work of healing the world.

Questions

Do you carry accusing voices in your head?

If so, how might they be silenced?

Breath Prayer

inhale: You have broken death's power.

exhale: There is no condemnation.

I couldn't help but laugh out loud
when I saw this [insight into God's defeat of evil].
My laughter was contagious,
and everyone who was in my room with me
began to laugh too.
The laughter made me so happy that I wished
everyone could see what I had seen
and join our laughter.

21

Let all who take refuge in you rejoice;
let them ever sing for joy.
Spread your protection over them,
so that those who love your name
may exult in you.

PSALM 5:11

Did you ever play Ha! when you were young? The rules go like this: Kids arrange themselves on the floor like a big crossword puzzle, each with their head on the stomach of another. The first kid says "ha," the second "ha ha," and so on. Heads start bouncing as air gets expelled from abdomens, and soon everyone dissolves into helpless hilarity.

Julian is not playing the game on her sickbed—and yet when she sees that Christ has fully defeated the Accuser, the joy that fills her makes her burst out in laughter. Heartfelt laughter is contagious, so those who are keeping watch in her room—probably her mother, perhaps her priest and some neighbors—can't help but laugh along, even though they haven't shared her revelations.

In J. R. R. Tolkien's *The Return of the King*, after the companions' great striving to rid the world of the Ring, Frodo and Sam fear that all is nevertheless lost. But then their wise guide Gandalf returns to them. Sam asks in wonder,

> "Is everything sad going to come untrue? What's happened to the world?"
>
> "A great Shadow has departed," said Gandalf, and then he laughed, and the sound was like music, or like water in a parched land; and as he listened the thought came to Sam that he had not heard laughter, the pure sound of merriment, for days upon days without count. It fell upon his ears like an echo of all the joys he had ever known.

This is the laughter that filled Julian when she realized evil has lost its power. Relief to the point of giddiness. Wonder like a thunderbolt. Absolute joy.

Questions

*How long has it been
since you were overcome with laughter?*

*Do you find Julian's confidence
in Christ's victory contagious?*

Breath Prayer

inhale: You have rescued us.

exhale: We are safe and free.

God's love created all things,
and Divine love keeps all things in existence,
and it shall keep everything forever.
Not one thing made shall ever be lost.

22

Yahweh is good to all,
and his compassion is over all that he has made....
Yahweh upholds all who are falling
and raises up all who are bowed down.
The eyes of all look to you,
and you give them their food in due season.
You open your hand,
satisfying the desire of every living thing.

PSALM 145:9, 14–16

In these passages, we return to God's love as our source of life and to that astounding word *all*. These words and ideas recur often in Julian's writing, as well as in the scriptures. Maybe that's because it takes a whole lifetime to fully integrate these realities, to know them in our bones.

Forever and *everything* further underline Julian's unconditional assertions—and notice the fivefold repetition of *all* in the verses from Psalm 145, along with *every* in the last verse. Julian's negation is significant too: *Not one thing made* will be missing. In the end, in the entire Creation, the category *lost* will be empty. In the meantime, God's mother love attends to us all, particularly when we are beaten down or falling.

In all Julian's "showings," "love was God's meaning." When we realize all things are created and held in Divine love, we begin to walk differently on the Earth. Everything becomes holy and worthy of care. We are not able to do all the necessary caring, since we are finite and in need of care ourselves. Still, we can participate in God's ongoing work of love, and we can hope for Creation's healing.

Questions

*What losses in your life or in the wider world
have been especially hard for you to accept?*

*Are you starting to believe
the "all and everything" promises?*

Breath Prayer

inhale: Our being is in God.

exhale: Nothing will be lost.

Resting in this Unity is the highest prayer,
and it reaches down to our deepest needs . . .
Think how neatly our food
is contained within our bodies,
is digested, and then is emptied out as needed,
like a lovely drawstring purse that opens and closes. . . .
All our bodies' natural functions are Divine vehicles,
filled with the love God bears us
whose souls are made in the Divine likeness.

23

The eye cannot say to the hand,
"I have no need of you,"
nor again the head to the feet,
"I have no need of you."
On the contrary, the members of the body
that seem to be weaker are indispensable,
and those members of the body
that we think less honorable
we clothe with greater honor,
and our less respectable members
are treated with greater respect....
God has so arranged the body,
giving the greater honor to the inferior member,
that there may be no dissension within the body,
but the members may have
the same care for one another.

1 Corinthians 12:21–25

My father was an unusual man: By the time I was in my teens, he was a missionary, university professor, psychotherapist, and pastor all at the same time. I will never forget the time he earnestly preached to our congregation about poop. (Read Deuteronomy 23:12–13 if you'd like to see his text.) Dad impressed upon us God's loving care for Hebrew soldiers in giving them instructions about proper hygiene when they were traveling and needed to relieve themselves. As far as I recall, the entire sermon focused on this point.

I confess I was delighted when I came upon a related point in Julian's writings. Julian focuses not on hygiene but on God's care in making us able to get rid of our body's waste in the first place. For a mystic and a theologian, Julian is beautifully earthy.

Releasing waste is "our [body's] deepest need" ("the lowest part of our need" in *TCJ*). Why would Julian focus on this aspect of God's care for us? Because she is getting ready to show us that Jesus, the Wisdom of God, bends low to be a Mother to us. And who is it that traditionally attends to babies' diapers, noticing whether the contents look healthy, cleaning the child with tenderness? Mothers. Jesus our Mother cares for our bodies, not just our spirits.

In Paul's extended metaphor of the church as Christ's body with many "members" (parts), when he writes of "less presentable" body parts, I believe he too is making a metaphor of the organs, muscles, and skin involved in excretion. But his point is more political: Society often looks down on the poor among us, the children, the disabled, those who struggle to survive, as being less important, people who can be forgotten and overlooked, even hidden out of sight. But just as all our body's parts, including our gastrointestinal systems, are necessary for our health, so our communities need each human's participation if society is to be healthy. In a healthy community, social hierarchies are upended, and the privileged find that the marginalized are essential.

Questions

*How do you feel knowing that
God loves even your private parts?*

*How can your community better honor
its "less presentable" members?*

Breath Prayer

inhale: You created this flesh.

exhale: Each body is a miracle.

The Trinity's high strength
is our Father,
the Trinity's deep Wisdom
is our Mother,
and the Trinity's great Love
is our Protector.
These Three are ours,
woven into the nature
and substance of our being.

24

When the Spirit of truth comes,
she will guide you into all the truth,
for she will not speak on her own
but will speak whatever she hears,
and she will declare to you
the things that are to come.
She will glorify me because she will take what is mine
and declare it to you.
All that the Father has is mine.

JOHN 16:13–15

Julian has a rich and deep Trinitarian theology. Her metaphors and titles for the Divine Persons are fresh yet completely in line with scripture.

Throughout the Gospels, Jesus often appeals to his relationship with his Father as the source of his authority to heal and to speak prophetically. He speaks of the Spirit as well, notably when reading Isaiah 61 in the Nazareth synagogue (Luke 4:16–19), but it's not until his upper-room discourse (John 13–17), just before his trial and crucifixion, that he begins pointing to the Spirit as a promise of God's presence and wisdom after he returns to the Father.

If I had been present for that final tender talk with the disciples, I would have wanted to ask questions to better understand the Divine interrelationships. I'd be a bit like Philip, who asked Jesus to show the Father to all of them! But I'm pretty sure Jesus would have answered me the same way he answered Philip: "Have I been with you so long, Ruth, and you still do not know me? Whoever has seen me has seen the Father" (John 14:8–9).

Meanwhile, Julian points to this simple mutual identity: We can call any of the three Persons Protector or Lover, Mother or Father, because they are inextricably one. We don't need to understand how this is so in order to swim in the eternal love that pulses among them.

What's more, Julian says, the Godhead's own life is somehow patterned within each human soul. We are structured to resemble our Source.

MEDITATIONS

Question

Are you experiencing God differently as you absorb Julian's delight in the Trinity?

Breath Prayer

inhale: Three in One . . .

exhale: You are tenderness and power.

The Go-Between is the Founder of the human family,
the Source of our nature and life,
from whom we all spring,
the Womb that encloses us all.
We shall all wind our way into this Go-Between,
finding there our total Heaven,
our everlasting joy.

25

In the beginning was the Word,
and the Word was with God,
and the Word was God. . . .
What has come into being in him was life,
and the life was the light of all people. . . .
To all who received him,
who believed in his name, he gave power
to become children of God,
who were born, not of blood or of the will of the flesh
or of the will of man, but of God.
And the Word became flesh and lived among us,
and we have seen his glory,
the glory as of a father's only son,
full of grace and truth.

JOHN 1:1–4, 12–14

After "Go-Between" and "Source" in the Julian excerpt, notice how quickly her language becomes familial. Look how she characterizes Jesus: as our originating Womb, as the One who sends us out into the adventure of life, as the One to whom we always return, who encloses us in safety and love. Here Julian is preparing the ground for a wonder-filled exploration of Jesus as our Mother.

John's Gospel also begins with high metaphor—God as the Word—but moves quickly into parental language: giving birth to light and life, human beings who are born of God, and then the Word in turn being born into flesh and manifesting the glory of the Creator's own Child.

Take a while to walk in and out of these images of birth, launching, return, and embrace. Jesus is our Go-Between who embodies and honors our full humanity, which includes our deification.

Questions

*How does it feel to know you
are genetically, biologically related to Jesus?*

*How would you like to grow
in honoring your body and others?*

Breath Prayer

inhale: We are born from you.

exhale: You are born in us.

Mother Christ
supports and hold us
in love within herself
(as a pregnant mother holds
her unborn child).

26

As a mother comforts her child,
so I will comfort you;
you shall be comforted in Jerusalem.

ISAIAH 66:13

Jesus carries us within himself in love. That's another modern English rendering (from *TCJ*) of the first part of Julian's sentence. This imagery of our intimacy with Christ is an icon for you and for me when we are feeling as if we float in the world without tethering.

Some of us have lost our biological parents to death or mental illness or estrangement. Some of us have no sisters or brothers to hold us in relationships of care and support. We lose friends too, we lose places and pets and familiar smells and voices. We may feel like strangers in the world, even among our closest friends when they have no response to our pain and anger. Perhaps they don't know how to respond, even though they love us; what moves us or frightens us doesn't seem to affect them. In so many ways, as humans, we are alone.

In the moments when this feeling is most sharp, it's hard but good to let ourselves feel it fully. When we consider the sense of separation and listen to the lonely child's voice inside us, then we can open ourselves to Christ's words in the silence of our being. We learn we are carried not only in Jesus's arms but inside Jesus himself. We learn our thoughts and emotions can be not merely a monologue but a dialogue. Someone hears our every cry.

As a pregnant mother holds her unborn child—a child who is longed for, an irreplaceable little one to nurture, cuddle, read to, and play music for—we are held by Mother Christ. We are known and deeply understood. We are tethered with a cord of love.

Questions

Where and when do you most often become aware of your aloneness?

Have you asked Jesus to meet you there?

Breath Prayer

inhale: Mother Jesus . . .

exhale: Hold me within yourself.

Our earthly mothers may not be able
to protect us from death
(no matter how much they long to),
but our Mother Jesus
will never allow her children to die.

27

*Can a woman forget her nursing child
or show no compassion for the child of her womb?
Even these might forget,
yet I will not forget you.*

ISAIAH 49:15

A couple I knew laughed as they told me about forgetting one of their daughters when it was time to depart from a visit to relatives. They had five children and a large van in which seatbelts were not regularly used. (I mention seatbelts because this lack was likely one of the reasons the little girl was left behind: The back seats swarmed with a mass of moving children, so it must have been easy to miss the littlest one. Also, this was before the days of cell phones.) It wasn't until they got home that they realized their mistake, and one of them drove back to get the forgotten child.

Jesus's mother and father had a similar experience when he was twelve. They didn't exactly *forget* him; they just assumed he was walking with friends in another part of the Nazareth crowd returning from a Jerusalem feast. A whole day passed before they realized he was missing. Then they searched for him frantically and hurried back to the city to find him. There he was, calmly discussing theology in the temple (Luke 2:41–51).

It's a great story, a sign of the identity Jesus was growing into—and apparently, he was not at all worried about being away from his human parents. He already knew God as his Parent. Mary and Joseph knew this as well, but they also knew Jesus was still dependent on human parental care and provision (even if he, like many twelve-year-olds, didn't quite realize it himself).

In Julian's understanding, Jesus is revealed as Mother of his own human mother. How lovely! The Hebrew scriptures also speak of God as maternal, as One who suffers in labor to bring us to birth, One who never gets distracted and leaves us behind, One who takes joy in us and sings over us.

And Jesus our Mother preserves our lives, so that ultimately, not one of us will be lost.

Questions

Have you tried addressing Jesus as Mother in your own prayers?

How does his motherhood speak healing to you?

Breath Prayer

inhale: You never forget us.

exhale: We're never lost to you.

In this way, our life is grounded
in Jesus, our True Mother,
in the foreseeing wisdom
that has no beginning or end.

28

*See, I have engraved you
on the palms of my hands.*

Isaiah 49:16

The mothering deficit I experienced as a child is probably why I'm so fond of Julian's vision of Jesus as our Mother. My mom was a person of integrity, talent, and love who had to take on too many responsibilities as a young adult. As a woman in a patriarchal church and society, she didn't have opportunities to exercise her gifts as she would have liked. Her relationship with my father underwent strains that were sometimes enormous. Almost certainly, she suffered from mild depression for long stretches. Meanwhile, I reminded Mom of Dad, whom I adored but whose weaknesses made her life challenging. No wonder I often wished for more tenderness and robust approval from her. Discovering that God could be approached as Mother was a great joy for me.

When my son was a baby, I learned the importance of the bonding gaze. A friend told me that breastfeeding is a perfect time to read, but once my son Graham was in my arms, I felt viscerally how life-giving our mutual gaze was.

I remember sitting on the floor one evening years later, leaning against a wall with my eyes closed, looking up with the eyes of my heart. As I exchanged a bonding gaze with God, God's eyes never turned away but held mine in great calm and love. My heavenly Mother did not find me difficult or triggering. She and I attached to one another in peace and mutual wonder.

Such bonding experiences did not mean I was a perfect mother myself. I have had to apologize to my children for periods in which I was absent too often and for hurtful things I said to them. Jesus is the only Mother who is steadfast, never averting her gaze, never lashing out.

Our life is grounded in Jesus, whose gaze on us never falters as he holds us in his scarred hands.

MEDITATIONS

Questions

*Try a bonding prayer—not speaking but gazing.
How does it feel?*

*How do your experiences of being parented,
and perhaps of parenting,
shape your relationship with Jesus?*

Breath Prayer

inhale: Mother Jesus . . .

exhale: Your gaze is my home.

When Christ took on human nature,
we too were conceived into life,
when he died on the cross
he birthed us into endless life,

and ever since and ever more,
he feeds us and nurtures us,
with a mother's gentle familiarity
as she cares for her children's
every intimate need.

29

And I, when I am lifted up from the earth,

will draw all people to myself.

JOHN 12:32

Bear with me when I say this: God the Parent did not send God the Son to die. At least not in the way a human father might choose to send his son, say, to fight in a war where he might not survive. Even less is God the Parent like an abusive human father who tortures his son or lets others do so. And yet sometimes, this is the impression our churches give us about why Jesus came to us.

Julian has helped me with this. Every action a member of a Trinity takes, she says, is chosen and carried out by all three Persons. Christ's incarnation was a Trinitarian act. And so was the cross. The Son *chose* it—and so did the Creator and the Spirit.

In Bethlehem, Divinity was born into the fragility of a tiny child of parents who had little to give but love; on the cross, God was born into an even deeper human vulnerability. The very human Jesus experienced a terrible sense of abandonment in those hours of excruciating physical pain, even though as God, he had chosen this surrender.

David Bentley Hart's translation of the Christian scriptures makes an intriguing point: In John 12:32, the Greek word rendered "draw" in most English translations is more accurately translated as "drag." This too speaks of the rough pain of childbirth: It takes a mighty effort to heave us into life. And this is a paradoxical birth that brings us *into* a strange and beautiful place, rather than ejecting us *from* a comfortable womb.

So, Julian repeats, the cross is our own birth into the life of God. We can understand it as she does, as a compelling confirmation that God is not only our Father, encouraging and correcting us as we move deeper into the life of faith. God is also our Mother who lets us inhabit her own body, feeding us with herself.

MEDITATIONS

Questions

If you take Communion (the Eucharist), bring this image of childbirth with you the next time. How does it change the experience?

Where in your life do you find Jesus feeding and nurturing you?

Breath Prayer

inhale: You breathe life into us.

exhale: You draw us to yourself.

The Divine Spirit is everything that is good,
everything that comforts us
and gives us pleasure.
This Spirit is our clothing.
In love, the Divine One wraps us up,
holds us close,
and encloses us with tenderness.

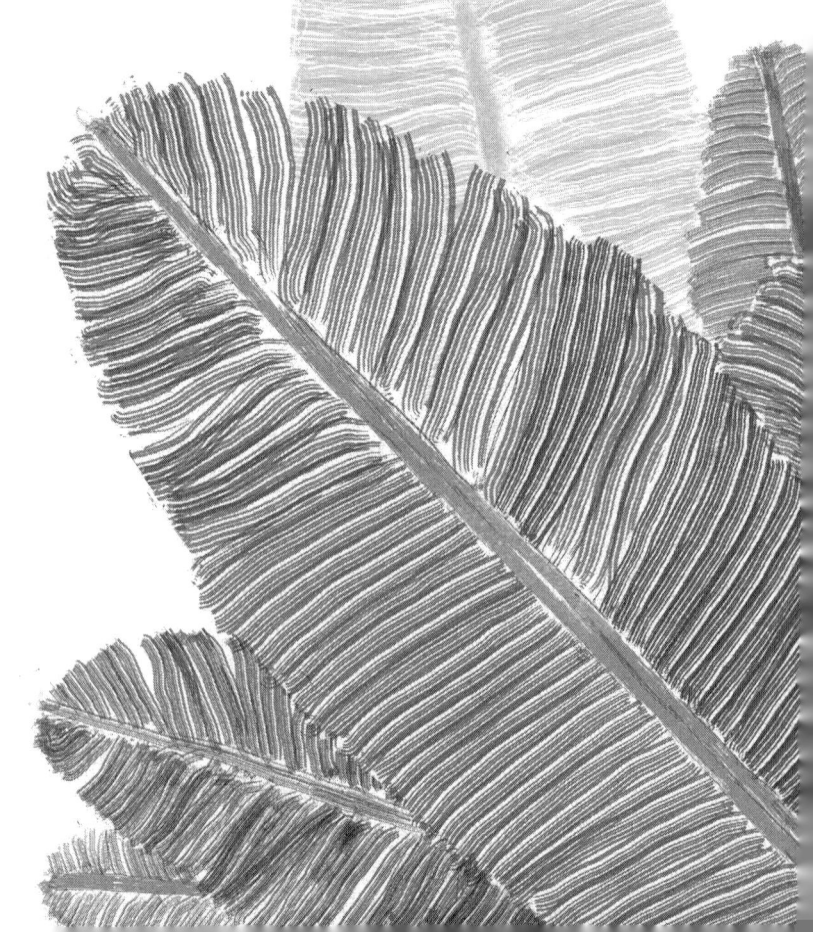

30

Put on the Lord Jesus Christ.

ROMANS 13:14

Julian often uses imagery of fabric and clothing when she writes of God's love for us. She takes a maternal tack with this biblical image of "putting on Christ." God is our clothing, the soft blanket we need to keep us warm and safe—and God is also the Mother who wraps and encloses us in love and holds us close. We can revel in this double metaphor for the intimacy it conveys: God next to our skin, God holding us tenderly.

The writer Amy Laura Hall, in her book about Julian titled *Laughing at the Devil,* can help us begin to grasp the same metaphor's sociopolitical depth. In medieval England, Hall explains, people in power were obsessed with status markers that could keep them distanced and protected from people of lower classes. Peasants, maids, farmers, different kinds of landowners, merchants, the divisions of clergy, nobility: *By law,* each group was assigned its own style of clothing so that each person could be visually classified and treated accordingly. These rules, called sumptuary laws, were intended to restrain the "lower classes" when it came to material luxury or extravagance.

And see how the Spirit pays no heed to them. How offensive to the aristocracy of Julian's day that a peasant digging rocks out of the soil could wear the same beautiful, comfortable garment as the most elegant noblewoman! In a similar way, when we look with the eyes of the heart at our own society, we realize that the runny-nosed child in a detention center at the border is wearing the same "Divine clothing" as the billionaire who considers outer space a tourist playground.

We all have the same social status in God's economy: *beloved.*

Questions

Do you treat others as though they were wearing Christ?

Do you regard yourself that way?

Breath Prayer

inhale: I am beloved.

exhale: I am wearing Christ.

For as the body is clad in the clothes,
and the flesh in the skin,
and the bones in the flesh,
and the heart in the breast,

so are we, soul and body,
wrapped in the goodness of God
and enclosed.

31

Therefore, as God's chosen ones,
holy and beloved,
clothe yourselves with compassion,
kindness, humility, meekness, and patience.
Bear with one another
and, if anyone has a complaint against another,
forgive each other;
just as the Lord has forgiven you,
so you also must forgive.
Above all, clothe yourselves with love,
which binds everything together
in perfect harmony.

Colossians 3:12–14

Julian's assertion that God layers us with clothing, wrapping us completely, takes my breath away. Her rhythmic listing of our physical layers—skin, flesh, bones, breast, heart—is absolute poetry, a song of our humanity. It makes me feel cozy, but much more, it makes me feel *safe* in the dizziness of being seen, known, and protected all the way to my core. The place where shame hides turns out to be a place where I am not shamed but held. My shame becomes a compost that nourishes compassion for myself and others.

One Sunday at church, when Colossians 3 was our text, an affirmation came to me: *This is a love I can wear.* I'm still committed to choosing this "clothing."

I've been using the first-person singular so far in this meditation—*I, me*—but look again at Julian's text and the words from Colossians. *We* is plural, *yourselves* is plural. The clothing, the wrapping, the deep safety are for us together in community, whether we are geographically near or far away from each other.

As I was finishing this book's writing, the Israeli military was pounding Gaza with bombs and artillery supplied by the United States. The vast majority of the victims were civilians, women and children. Many Americans, distraught, wrote to our elected officials to object. Some of us went out in the street or interrupted political fundraisers to say that the carnage had to stop, that military aid had to stop.

During that time, when I went to church, I brought that pain—that compassion—with me. I found myself wanting to sing all the hymns and worship songs with Gaza in mind. I changed *I* to *we*, *me* to *us* as I sang. "We lift our eyes up unto the mountains: / where does our help come from? . . . Oh how we need you, Lord, / you are our only hope."

The clothing in which God wraps us is for us to share with others, to drape over the shoulders of the lonely, to send with our voices across the world to Gaza and Ukraine, Congo and Myanmar. Together, we sing a song of suffering-with, of being-with. We choose to clothe ourselves in love and in necessary hope.

Questions

What does it mean for your shame to be clothed in not-shame?

Where does your heart want to find a way to share the clothing of love?

Breath Prayer

inhale: Strengthen us to wear you.

exhale: Mother God, wrap us all.

We should take great joy
in the fact that God
lives in our souls—
and even more joy in the fact
that our souls live in God!
Our souls were created
to be God's home;
and our souls' home is God.

32

You who live in the shelter of the Most High,
who abide in the shadow of the Almighty,
will say to Yahweh, "My refuge and my fortress;
my God, in whom I trust."

Psalm 91:1

God is our home—not merely in the sense of "hometown," where we might return to visit, but as our dwelling place, habitat, where we spend our time, our whole lives. God is our identity: not a consumer identity, a self-presentation based on our choices and our desire to please, but our deepest, most essential identity that springs from our physical and spiritual DNA, the Source of our being.

And yes, our physical DNA is included in our divine identity. Many religious traditions, including Christianity, have had a body-denigrating understanding of the spiritual life. But Julian says her visions showed her "our spiritual essence can be rightly called our soul—but at the same time, our sensual natures are also our soul" (chap. 56). It's rather like the Trinity: Our relationship to God is enriched as we contemplate the three separate Persons, but in another way, they are indistinguishable because God is One.

In recent decades, brain science has emphasized for me the impossibility of separating mind from body, soul from spirit. Yet at times, we all experience feelings of self-alienation, a mistrust of our bodies or the workings of our minds. The word *mystery* applies to the created human self just as it does to the uncreated God.

God never undergoes such alienation—or does she? Remember Jesus's anguished prayer in Gethsemane: "Let this cup pass, if it be your will" (see Matthew 26:36–46; Mark 14:32–42). The suffering Jesus was about to experience was chosen in the perfect unity of the Godhead, yet in his humanity, Jesus wished it could be avoided. God intimately understands the painful divisions we experience within ourselves.

Being at home in God can feel strange. We naturally bring along with us the misdirection and twisted motives we were used to in our human family of origin; at first, we automatically assume they are also part of our deeper

God-home. We can't quickly dislodge trauma from the grooves of our brains.

As we dwell in God, however, peace and encouragement and unconditional love become more familiar. This is the source of our deepest identity. This is what we were made for.

Question

*Contrast Psalm 90's picture of
our God-home with the one in Psalm 91.
Have you experienced both?*

Breath Prayer

inhale: You hold me always.

exhale: You are my home.

The soul does
what it was made for:
it sees God,
it grasps God,
it loves God.

33

As a deer longs for flowing streams,
so my soul longs for you, O God.
My soul thirsts for God,
for the living God.
When shall I come and behold
the face of God? . . .
By day Yahweh commands steadfast love,
and at night God's song is with me,
a prayer to the God of my life.

PSALM 42:1–2, 8

Our natural state, Julian says, is closeness to God. I am grateful for her hopefulness. I was brought up to mistrust my own soul, to believe that it was inherently alienated from God.

According to the "miserable sinner" brand of theology, babies are born tainted with evil (though they're not held responsible until the "age of accountability"). When I look back, a lot of what the church told me was "evil" involved perfectly normal (though sometimes obnoxious) behaviors related to stages of human development. Still, no one can deny that human carelessness and active wrongdoing have wreaked great harm in our world.

Both original-sin and original-blessing beliefs need nuance if they are to be in line with a biblical understanding of human life, the best psychological and neuroscience research, and our own experience. Julian offers us this nuance as she emphasizes that we are made for closeness to God, and no matter how skewed our thinking and behaviors may become, our souls are always seeking God, whether we realize it or not. Neurological research in recent decades confirms that our sense of well-being and our empathy for others grow as we practice deep prayer and meditation. (For Christians, this may look like contemplation, centering prayer, *lectio divina*, or repetition of the Jesus Prayer.) As we become aware of God, as we seek God consciously, we flourish as persons. We become more ourselves.

The beautiful verses from Psalm 42 that began this meditation were written within a context of distress and tumult.

The psalmist reminds us that in times of trouble, we can remember we are anchored in Mother God's lovingkindness. We are cherished and forgiven. She sings a lullaby to us in the night, drawing us back into our primal state of Divine nearness and shelter.

This is what we are made for.

Questions

Have you been aware of your hunger for God— or is it hard to access?

What difference might you feel realizing that other people are hungering for God too?

Breath Prayer

inhale: Your love holds me.

exhale: I keep my eyes on you.

Our souls are rooted so deeply in God,
where they are so endlessly treasured,
that we cannot truly know them
until we first know God, the Soul-Maker,
with whom our souls are oned . . .
The Divine Being is nearer to us than our own souls . . .

We can never come to full knowledge of God
until we first know clearly our own souls.

34

*[Jesus] called the crowd with his disciples
and said to them, "If any wish to come after me,
let them deny themselves
and take up their cross and follow me.
For those who want to save their life will lose it,
and those who lose their life for my sake,
and for the sake of the gospel, will save it.
For what will it profit them
to gain the whole world and forfeit their life?
Indeed, what can they give in return for their life?"*

MARK 8:34–37

The King James Version of the Bible that I grew up with uses *soul* in these verses, whereas a modern translation of Mark 8 uses *life*. That translation reinforces the understanding that the soul is not an esoteric part of the person that must be clearly differentiated from the body or spirit.

In my youth, Christian adults often quoted this saying of Jesus to urge us to leave behind the creature comforts of North American affluence and become missionaries in the "Third World." Indeed, my own parents heeded that call, which is why I spent most of my childhood and adolescence in Colombia instead of the United States. (I'm forever grateful for the rich cross-cultural life I was given.)

Notice that Jesus is not calling us to despise our lives or our souls. In Julian's words, God "endlessly treasures" our souls—and it's *for this reason*, Jesus says, that we must surrender them. Paradoxically, our souls are preserved as we put our lives at risk to follow the Way of Jesus.

There's another paradox in Julian's words: Do we learn about ourselves by contemplating God—or do we learn about God by first being students of our souls? She does not try to resolve these seemingly contradictory admonishments, because if we're diligent and honest, both will lead us to the same place. God's life is patterned in ours: Like Jesus, we will have a cross to bear—the cost involved in resisting the world's system—yet we are also held firm in a bedrock of eternal love.

You are endlessly treasured. That's why you can break society's rules to enact justice. That's why you can sing as you are handcuffed and led away to jail. This is one way in which you are like Jesus. The empire cannot take away your soul.

Questions

What are some hazards of "losing our lives" for Jesus?

How can we protect each other in the work of justice and generosity?

Breath Prayer

inhale: We are treasured.

exhale: We can give ourselves away.

Our souls are knit tightly to God
at the deepest level of their being,
with a knot so delicate and strong
that our souls are [oned] to God,
made endlessly whole and clean and safe.

35

*There is now no condemnation
for those who are in Christ Jesus.*

ROMANS 8:1

Julian says we are *knit* and *oned* to God, *enclosed* in God. (Ellyn Sanna uses the more modern, Latin-rooted *unite*, but I find the Middle English *oned*, which Julian herself used, to be more concrete.) The apostle Paul loves to say we are *in Christ*. It's a whole family of related metaphors.

I rather wish we had retained Paul's habit of referring to people who were on the Jesus Way as being "in Christ." For example, in Romans 16:7, he says that Andronicus and Junia "were in Christ before I was." This language of being *in* originated with Jesus: "On that day you will know that I am in my Father, and you in me, and I in you," he tells his closest friends (John 14:20) shortly before his death and resurrection.

Doesn't this open the door to in-groups and out-groups, reminding us unpleasantly of middle school and high school, when belonging to the right peer group was of utmost importance? Remarkably perhaps (since Christians today can be very focused on who is in and who is out), it doesn't work that way for Jesus, Paul, or Julian.

Of course, Jesus had harsh words for some people of his day—but mainly his criticisms were directed at the rich and privileged who themselves were exclusionary. Paul, too, tended to focus his ire on those who wanted to restrict the circle of God's chosen to people who observed Jewish ceremonial rules. As for Julian, she does not worry at all about defining an out-group: All of us are "we," she insists; we are all in God, and we are all knitted and oned to God. And she wants us to know that because of this oneing at our core, we are endlessly made and kept holy and whole.

No condemnation.

How would we live and act in the world if we were sure of this? How *will* we live and act?

Question

How does it feel to be fastened so securely to God?

Breath Prayer

inhale: I am in you.

exhale: You have oned me to yourself.

We are God's joy and God's delight—

and God is our medicine and our life.

36

Do not fear, for you will not be ashamed;
do not be discouraged,
for you will not suffer disgrace, . . .
For the mountains may depart
and the hills be removed,
but my steadfast love shall not depart from you,
and my covenant of peace shall not be removed,
says Yahweh, who has compassion on you.

ISAIAH 54:4–10

This part of Isaiah's beautiful prophecy is addressed to discouraged Jewish exiles longing to return to their homeland. We can sit with these same words now, and see if they surround us with the confidence we need to face things that embarrass us or make us feel shame.

Recently, after a vivid dream, I felt called to be more vulnerable, not only with other people but also with myself. God is calling me to face the shame I carry about my work (disappointing book sales), my body (recent weight gain), my tendency to stay comfortably at home and write rather than go out in the streets when major social injustices require protest. You could likely make your own list. The point is not to feel further shame about being ashamed! Rather, the Spirit calls us to listen to and befriend those parts of ourselves that are mired in dishonor and embarrassment, so that we can let them soak in Divine love as we move into greater freedom.

In *The Sound of Life's Unspeakable Beauty*, author Martin Schleske encourages us with his interpretation of this reality:

> We have each been entrusted to ourselves, and with God's mindset, we can see our soul as a friend and say: "Look, my friend, you are beautiful!" (see Song of Solomon 4:1). But this requires work and understanding.

Seeing myself as a friend helps me emerge from self-rejection.

Shame may be rooted in abuse committed against us or in unreasonable social expectations. It may reflect our own failures and sins. But regardless of its source, Julian's radiant understanding is that delight—the opposite of shame—is Mother God's response to us.

And God's delight heals our shame. It moves us toward liberation.

Questions

What shame do you carry?

If God is for you, who will be against you?

Breath Prayer

inhale: Anchored in your love . . .

exhale: I see and love my hidden self.

Our souls sit at rest in God,
our souls stand up straight in God's strength,
and our souls' very natures are rooted
in God's endless love.

37

As you therefore have received Christ Jesus the Lord, continue to walk in him, rooted and built up in him and established in the faith, just as you were taught, abounding in thanksgiving.

Colossians 2:6–7

As I was in the midst of writing these meditations about each human soul's attachment to God, I awoke sad and angry nearly every morning. It was as if I'd been fighting—and not winning—some battle in my dreams. Practices that normally soothe me (such as walking, clearing the sink of dishes, baking bread) didn't help much.

One evening, I attended an organizing meeting to extend our advocacy for Gaza, where I found new folks ready to contribute energy and vision. I was immensely encouraged.

A friend had given me a ride to and from the meeting, and our conversation in the car also fed my soul.

But the next morning I awoke unhappy again. I tried to use the day well. I did laundry and scrubbed things and walked more than a mile to return a book to the library. I picked up a few bits of trash that had blown into our yard. I gazed at the red and gold tulips in my garden that were blooming fiercely. And still, I couldn't find release from the loneliness and shame that felt hooked into my muscles and my heart.

Finally, I sat down to think and write, and I remembered an encounter from the night before. To open the ceasefire meeting, I offered a prayer, and later, a young woman who was new to the group approached me. "Thank you for praying to Mother God!" she said. "I had never heard anyone do that, and it touched me. I'm going to call God *Mother* in my prayers from now on!"

The memory of her words helped me become aware of what I most needed: my Mother's kindness. Not knowing exactly what to pray, I opened up my vaguely remembered dreams, the shame and the anger—and then I waited. God looked at me with great tenderness. She knows how much I love my solitude and also how painful it is at times. She sees the shame I feel about my aloneness and, at the same time, about not being perfectly self-sufficient. Oh, and also the shame I feel about fussing over my little struggles while a terrible genocide is being carried out in Palestine!

Her eyes do not accuse. She only loves.

Mother Lord—my term of endearment for Jesus—is present with me in every moment of exhaustion and vulnerability. And with you likewise. Often, she offers no solution, just her enfolding presence.

As we are shaken by pain, shame, confusion, our Mother trusts you and me to put down roots ever deeper in Love. We can stand, and we can rest, because we are always held.

Question

Is it hard to open up to God things you are not proud of?

Breath Prayer

inhale: You've got the whole world . . .

exhale: In your hands.

So I both saw God
and at the same time I longed to see God.

                                          I had God
                                    even as I yearned for God.

This is the way our lives go,
that is the way they are meant to go,
while we are in this life.

38

O God, you are my God; I seek you;
my soul thirsts for you;
my flesh faints for you,
as in a dry and weary land
where there is no water. . . .
My soul is satisfied as with a rich feast,
and my mouth praises you with joyful lips
when I think of you on my bed
and meditate on you in the watches of the night,
for you have been my help,
and in the shadow of your wings I sing for joy.

Psalm 63:1, 5–7

The lyricist writes of immense hunger for God and immense satisfaction, all in the same psalm. And Julian says both are healthy and normal for us as we grow as human beings, as embodied souls.

So many of the meditations in this book point to the finding of God, the satisfaction as we relax into the quiet of Mother God's nearness, her heartbeat. But sometimes, we are far from that satisfaction, even when we're committed to living in God's presence and being open to the Spirit. We are busy with a tangle of obligations: work deadlines; cleaning; errands; home repairs and vehicle repairs; childcare, elder care, or pet care; studies; health-related appointments. During some seasons of our lives, even painting, making music, writing, or carrying out urgently needed actions for justice feels dry and uninspired. And prayer feels dry too.

That's normal, Julian says—and all the great mystics agree. Our sense of dryness doesn't mean God is any farther away. It doesn't mean we're being unfaithful or have stopped loving Jesus. It simply means we're finite: We're incapable of remaining at a high emotional or spiritual pitch. It may also signify that as we are going through trials, we're being invited to grow in patience, perseverance, and hope. We are normal created beings, who sometimes live in bright light and sometimes in shadows.

This is the way our lives go; this is the way they are meant to go. Guarding time for spiritual disciplines like prayer, sacred reading, worship, and silence will serve us even when these things don't feel rewarding. Knowing that God is always listening to us encourages us to listen back. Sometimes we hear God's words of love. Sometimes we just hear silence.

Questions

*What memories do you have
of deep satisfaction in God's nearness?*

What have the times of need and longing taught you?

Breath Prayer

inhale: Your silence is not abandonment.

exhale: In my hunger, you are near.

God's love creates in us
such a unity that we cannot
separate ourselves
from each other.

39

Speaking the truth in love,
we must grow up in every way into him
who is the head, into Christ,
from whom the whole body, joined
and knit together by every ligament
with which it is equipped,
as each part is working properly,
promotes the body's growth
in building itself up in love.

EPHESIANS 4:15–16

Julian's primary focus is the soul's relationship with God, not relationships among members of human communities. But as we've seen, the high honor she gives to the individual soul has powerful implications for how we live and deal with each other. And sometimes, as in the quote on page 170, she directly addresses our social-spiritual selves.

"You are my favorite second daughter," my father used to say, pulling me onto his lap. Wishing I were *the* favorite, I argued, "But Daddy, I'm your *only* second daughter." Dad treated my siblings exactly the same way, holding each one and naming some things that were special about them. I'm grateful for Dad's modeling of family unity and the way it undermined our sibling rivalry. To this day, my siblings are my closest friends.

In this way, Dad was a lot like God, who gives us a sense of our unique importance and lets us know we are cherished, while never implying that other people are less beloved. This helps us grow toward maturity within our family, our faith community, and the broader world.

The apostle Paul often focused on teaching fledgling Jesus-followers to care for each other, living counter to the ways of the Roman Empire. We belong to each other, he says, and we will grow up *together* as we are nurtured and guided by Christ. Notice how the sentence that stretches from verse 15 to 16 of Ephesians 4 begins and ends with love. And there's Julian's beloved word *knit*. The love that unites us with God also binds us to each other.

I have encountered too much abuse in Christian communities to be sanguine about the possibility of such unity. I have needed to separate myself from some people who were doing me harm, and you probably have too. Still, we belong to each other irrevocably in the sense that when one part of the social body is unhealthy, all parts suffer. My healing is bound up in others' healing and flourishing.

This is why we, as people of faith and as citizens of larger communities, need to listen to prison and police abolitionists. Can we imagine new, hopeful structures that will still protect the vulnerable, while giving those who have harmed others a path toward restitution and transformation?

Questions

How has unity with others been fractured in your life?

Where have you experienced the reknitting of social belonging?

Breath Prayer

inhale: Mother of peace . . .

exhale: Heal our brokenness.

All souls kept safe everywhere
are eternally rescued by this same knot,
[oned in the oneing],
made whole and healthy
through Divine health.

40

Husbands should love their wives
as their own bodies.
He who loves his wife loves himself.
For no one ever hates his own flesh,
but he nourishes and tenderly cares for it,
just as Christ does for the church,
because we are members of his body.
"For this reason a man will leave
his father and mother
and be joined to his wife,
and the two will become one flesh."
This is a great mystery,
but I am speaking about Christ and the church.

EPHESIANS 5:28–32

If you have suffered in marriage, as I have, take a deep breath: This meditation will *not* focus on marriage.

As we have already seen, Julian often uses *one* as a verb, first for the uniting of the soul with God, and then for God's creatures' becoming one with each other. Both Julian's words and the apostle Paul's have multiple meanings. We need them all.

In these passages, Julian and Paul offer us blindingly beautiful visions of the meaning and effect of oneing between human beings. Paul quotes the Genesis 2 Creation story to remind men in the patriarchal society of his day that women and men are originally of the same flesh (Eve was differentiated from an originally androgynous Adam), and thus they are not opposites but kindred bodies and souls. The husband's calling to live out this oneness with his spouse is just one example of the mutual submission that is the Jesus Way (see the proper introduction to this passage in Ephesians 5:21). If we are not married, we are still part of the human oneing that is patterned after—and flowing from—our oneness with the Trinity.

In the cosmos of Creation, we all belong and are knitted together, whether we recognize it or not: not just humans to humans, but also humans to trees to wolves to fungi to butterflies to oceans and all the lives that dwell therein. Even to space and other planets. In the new Earth—the fulfillment of all things—that oneing will be a source of everlasting joy.

These insights are deep enough for us to swim in for a long time. For example, our social interdependence is a given, and our primal hunger is to belong. Yet where there is no justice, our belonging to each other can feel like a curse. Our oneing with fellow creatures is also a given, but we violate it when our way of life destroys forests and animal species.

In the breath prayer below, consider how we breathe in oxygen exuded by the plants around us, and then we exhale carbon dioxide, which helps them in turn.

Questions

What steps can we take toward greater wholeness— holiness—right now?

How can we better acknowledge and live in our ties to each other?

Breath Prayer

inhale: I take in your oxygen.

exhale: I send my breath to you.

I believe on the Last Day,
the Trinity shall accomplish
an amazing deed.
We will never know what that deed is
until it is accomplished. . . .
The Great Deed was
planned out from the beginning
and hidden within the Divine Essence,
and by it shall absoluutely
everything be made well.

For just as the joyful Trinity made
everything out of nothing,
so the same Trinity can make
well all that is not well.

41

See, the home of God is among mortals.
He will dwell with them;
they will be his peoples,
and God himself will be with them and be their God;
he will wipe every tear from their eyes.
Death will be no more;
mourning and crying and pain will be no more,
for the first things have passed away.

REVELATION 21:3–4

Julian writes these "spoiler" sentences—letting us in on how the Story of Time is fulfilled—in chapter 32, fairly early in the *Revelations of Divine Love*. I have saved them for the near-end of *Dearworthy* partly because I love saving the best for last, but also because I don't want to imply that our hope is *only* for the new Heaven and new Earth. Some people used to say that the call to "get saved" to avoid hellfire and get on the

Heaven-approved list was just "pie in the sky by and by." That's not what Julian's talking about. We're called to hope for our own time, to take steps toward personal growth and social justice.

Yet we need an ultimate hope too. Throughout all the decades of my life, as I have sought to participate in the good work God is doing to redeem the world, I have had many moments of awe and beauty; I've also had many disappointments. When I first read Julian's words about the Great Deed, my body told me I'd encountered something awe-ful, something amazing: I gasped and chills ran through me. Julian promises that this world's work will eventually be complete, that Revelation 21—which also brings on chills each time I read it—will be fulfilled, and every tear wiped away.

It will take a Great Deed to make all things well. In the Incarnation and the cross, God has already entered the world's suffering. In the Resurrection, Jesus showed that death will be vanquished. But the consummation of all things is still to come.

Will the last judgment be a moment of soberness but also joy? Perhaps Mother God will invite us with great compassion to review our lives; she will urge us into the full transformation that will strengthen us to live in the Beloved Community. I wonder if the lowest in worldly standing will go first and then turn around, calling the rest of us to follow. Perhaps we will be so grateful to be welcomed that competition and priority will not even enter our minds. Those whose souls have rotted from their oppression of others will be offered tasks of service and restitution, so that they too will be oned to God and the holy community. Perhaps the children of Gaza will lead us all in a dance of liberation.

If I believe in God at all—and I do—it's a God whose love is vastly greater than mine, whose imagination for how all things can be healed is far beyond my own.

If you find it hard to believe this, do not be ashamed. For right now, let me believe for you that Mother God is set on earning your trust, and she will go about it with great patience. We have all been wounded, and our souls' healing does not follow an external timetable. If you still doubt, let me believe for you that you are loved beyond reason.

Questions

What healing—of another person or thing or of your own— are you still waiting for?

What do you want to say to God about that?

Breath Prayer

inhale: Come . . . come . . . come . . . come . . .

exhale: To heal and make all things new.

Do you really want to know
the Protector's meaning in the showings?
Well then, learn it well.
Love was God's meaning.
Who showed you these visions? Love.
What was shown? Love.
Why were you shown these visions? For love.
Hold on to that love.

42

God is love,
and those who abide in love abide in God,
and God abides in them.

1 JOHN 4:16

Love is our home. Love is our reason.

Meditating on the Trinity, we come to understand that love is not just something God does. Love is what God *is*. The three Persons abide in a dance of love, gazing at each other with joy.

And we are created out of that love. We exist because God is love. We are stitched to Divinity. No matter how lost we feel, God does not let go of us. Awareness of our origin centers us. We are oned with God.

This is a union, a belonging, that moves in both directions. Our innate desire lifts us toward God, the way plants rise toward light. And through the Incarnation and the cross, we come to see that God has always been seeking us. The Divine chose to join us in human limitation and suffering, even death. Because of love.

Because we are God's children and God's lovers, we also reach toward each other in love. Love is patterned into us. Most of us must work hard to learn to love well, but the Spirit of Love is with us to help. As we grow, we become free to give ourselves away.

Sometimes our freedom involves tending to our own wounds or accepting others' loving care. We learn to love ourselves too, because God loves us.

When we need to confront violence against ourselves or others, love enables us to choose nonviolent resistance as our response, just as Jesus did. Violence can be ingenious, but it is never creative. Nonviolent resistance is wildly creative: It might involve singing or planting olive trees or lying down in the middle of an intersection or offering a loaf of bread or writing a letter or chaining oneself to a fence or praying for rain or . . .

Deliberate nonviolence disarms. It surprises. It loves.

Our love is rooted in God's love. Love shapes us into persons who love.

Questions

Does your soul know it is fastened to Love?

What daily practices help you abide in Love?

Breath Prayer

inhale: You are my reason.

exhale: You are my home.

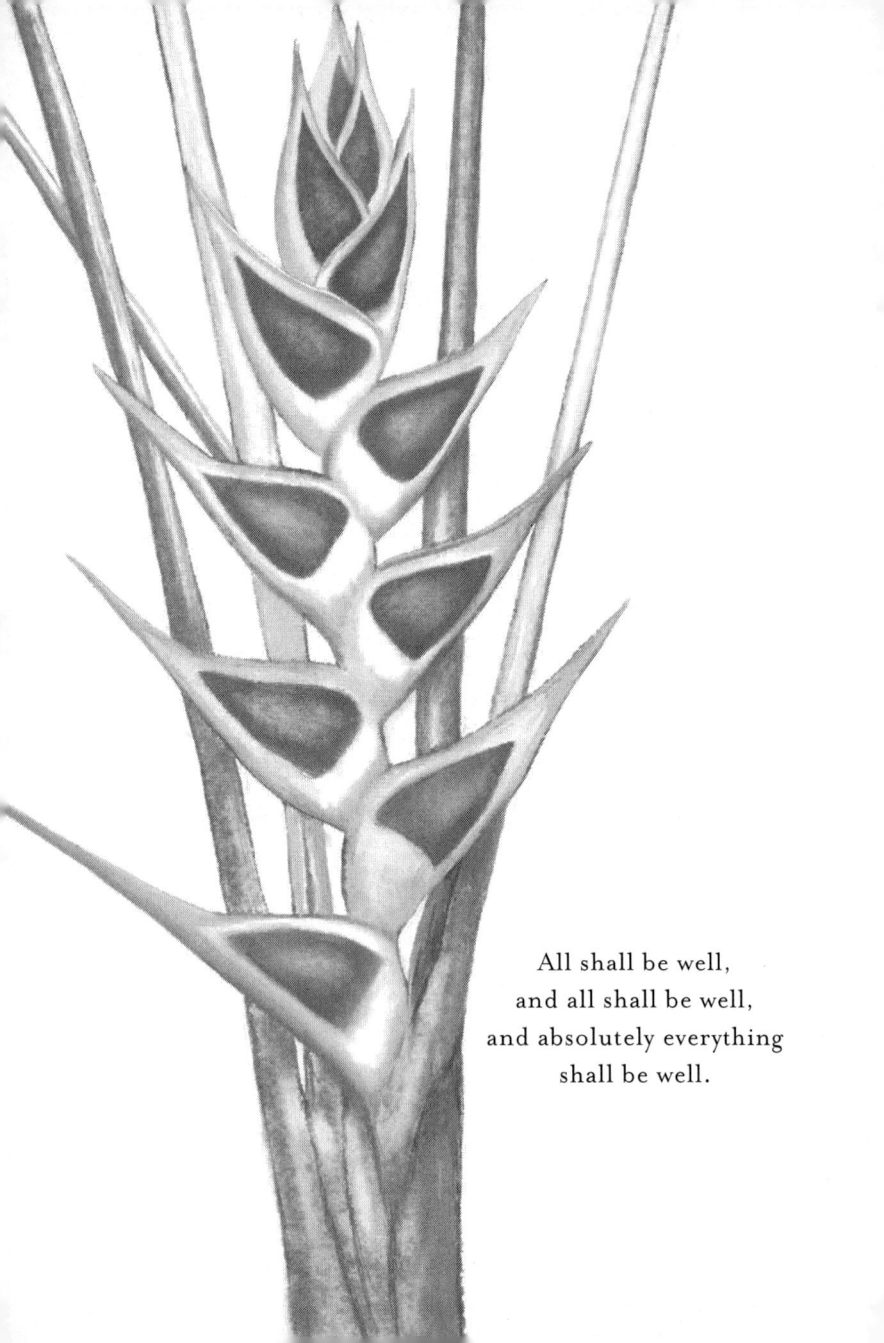

All shall be well,
and all shall be well,
and absolutely everything
shall be well.

REPRISE

If God is for us, who is against us?
He who did not withhold his own Son
but gave him up for all of us,
how will he not with him also give us everything else?
Who will bring any charge against God's elect?
It is God who justifies. Who is to condemn?
It is Christ who died, or rather, who was raised,
who is also at the right hand of God,
who also intercedes for us.
Who will separate us from the love of Christ?
Will affliction or distress or persecution
or famine or nakedness or peril or sword? . . .

*No, in all these things we are more than victorious
through him who loved us.
For I am convinced that neither death,
nor life, nor angels, nor rulers, nor things present,
nor things to come, nor powers,
nor height, nor depth,
nor anything else in all creation
will be able to separate us from the love of God
in Christ Jesus our Lord.*

ROMANS 8:31–39

Julian's early showings include strange and gruesome visions of Jesus's sufferings on the cross. I am not drawn to those images, but Julian found them marvelous and comforting. I think she, like the first disciples, was able to believe God's assurances of wellness—well-being and restoration of all that is damaged—because she had seen Jesus suffering with us.

The healing of all things does not involve a magic wand. It's not the detached action of a god playing a cosmic game. Jesus suffered real damage just as we do. The need for things to be well is *personal* for Julian's Protector.

All shall be well, and all shall be well. And absolutely everything—*all manner of thing*, as Julian rendered it—shall be well.

Oh child, Mother God says. *Your desire is not too much for me. You don't even know how much and how many things need to be set right, to be brought into wellness. It is more than you can ask or imagine. I promise you, though, that restoration is for all. Not just for humans, not even just for creatures that breathe.*

Every kind of every thing shall be well.

Questions

In what ways is my life a sign of the coming restoration?

How does my community point to full and joyful wellness?

Breath Prayer

inhale: Your kingdom come.

exhale: Your will be done.

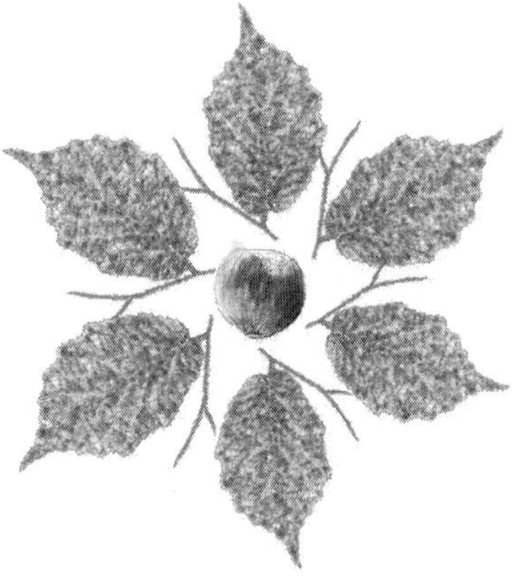

SOURCES & FURTHER READING

Nearly all my Julian texts come from Ellyn Sanna's *All Shall Be Well: A Modern-Language Version of the Revelation of Julian of Norwich* (Vestal, NY: Anamchara Books, 2018). The texts for meditations 3 and 34, as well as any others in the text marked *TCJ*, are from *The Complete Julian of Norwich*, edited and translated by John-Julian, OJN (Brewster, MA: Paraclete, 2009). Paraclete granted permission for me to alter these texts lightly, mainly changing capitalization and avoiding masculine pronouns for God (but not for Jesus). I've made a few similar changes to Sanna's version, most notably, substituting "oned" or "oneing" where she used the words "united" or "uniting." Sanna also chose in many cases to translate the Middle English *wel* with the word "good," where I have chosen to revert to "well."

Invitation

Amy Frykholm, *Julian of Norwich: A Contemplative Biography* (Brewster, MA: Paraclete, 2010). I recommend two compelling recent historical novels about Julian as well: Victoria Mackenzie, *For Thy Great Pain Have Mercy on My Little Pain* (London: Bloomsbury, 2023), and Claire Gilbert, *I, Julian* (London: Hodder & Stoughton, 2023).

Meditation 3

Amy Frykholm, "Julian the Theologian," *Christian Century*, May 2023, https://www.christiancentury.org/article/features/julian-theologian.

Meditation 4

Find a handy list of "all/everyone/world" scriptures at *The Internet Monk Archives*: https://imonk.blog/2020/08/05/92833/. Or read meditation 2 in David Bentley Hart, *That All Shall Be Saved: Heaven, Hell, and Universal Salvation* (New Haven, CT: Yale University Press, 2019). Hart also shows, by the way, that in the first centuries of the church, most Christians did not believe hell was a permanent destiny for anyone. About Hart's book more generally:

It was an important read for me, though Hart is impatient, even insulting, about "infernalists" who continue to insist the Bible teaches eternal conscious torment for those who did not choose to follow Jesus in this life. If you'd prefer a more approachable book, try one I'm just starting to explore: Sharon L. Baker, *Razing Hell: Rethinking Everything You've Been Taught about God's Wrath and Judgment* (Louisville, KY: Westminster John Knox, 2010).

Meditation 9

Katharine Hayhoe is a Christian climate scientist who keeps a careful eye on the data, both positive and negative, and encourages us to hold hope for the Earth. I encourage you to listen to her TED talk, which is pinned on the Posts page of her website, katharinehayhoe.com, and follow her on social media.

Meditation 10

See Sharon D. Welch, *A Feminist Ethic of Risk* (Minneapolis: Fortress, 2000), on developing an ethical stance to draw us out of the helpless feeling that we can do nothing to respond to large social problems.

Meditation 11

"Wealth Distribution in the United States in the Third Quarter of 2023," Statista, https://www.statista.com/statistics/203961/wealth-distribution-for-the-us/.

Meditation 15

U.S. Fish and Wildlife Service, "Insects," in ECOS: Environmental Conservation Online System, https://ecos.fws.gov/ecp/report/species-listings-by-tax-group?statusCategory=Listed&groupName=Insects; also "Rhadine infernalis," Wikipedia.

Meditation 18

This image of being cheek to cheek in darkness came to me when I was reading Fr. Thomas Green's beautiful book *When the Well Runs Dry: Prayer Beyond the Beginnings* (Notre Dame, IN: Ave Maria, 1979). When he says, "The darkness is not because God is so far away but because he is so close" (p. 111), he is summarizing St. John of the Cross's teaching about the dark night of the soul. Fr. Green's own image is of praying in a dimly lit chapel: if someone comes in and suddenly switches on the main lights, we are blinded, not because of a lack of light but because there is so much. Green's book is instructive at a deep level, and reassuring for the serious pray-er who is distressed because their experience of prayer has become dry. Be aware, though, that its language is a bit old-fashioned even for its time, with *man* frequently used for *person*. Green draws frequently on Teresa of Ávila as well as John of the Cross, so this is a good resource if you're wanting an introduction to these classical mystical writers.

Meditation 21

J. R. R. Tolkien, *The Return of the King* (New York: Ballantine Books, 1965), 283.

Meditation 25

A clear explanation of deification, with lots of biblical references, is available here: Mark Shuttlesworth, "Theosis: Partaking of the Divine Nature," Antiochian Christian Orthodox Christian Diocese of North America (n.d.), http://ww1.antiochian.org/content/theosis-partaking-divine-nature.

Meditation 29

David Bentley Hart, *The New Testament: A Translation* (New Haven, CT: Yale University Press, 2017), 200.

Meditation 30

Find a powerful exploration of God as our clothing in Lauren Winner, *Wearing God: Clothing, Laughter, Fire, and Other Overlooked Ways of Meeting God* (San Francisco: HarperOne, 2016).

I drew mainly from page 21 of Amy Laura Hall's book *Laughing at the Devil: Seeing the World with Julian of Norwich* (Durham, NC: Duke University Press, 2018), but she has powerful insights related to sumptuary laws elsewhere too; consult her index.

Meditation 33

In 2014, Rob Moll published a beautiful little book summarizing recent research along these lines: *What Your Body Knows About God: How We Are Designed to Connect, Serve, and Thrive* (Downers Grove, IL: InterVarsity Press).

Meditation 34

"We can never come to full knowledge of God until we first know clearly our own soul" is quoted from *TCJ*.

SOURCES & FURTHER READING

Meditation 35

In an attempt to demonstrate that despite her expansive view of salvation, she is faithful to the teachings of the Roman Catholic Church, Julian lists (in chapter 34) the people the church teaches are going to hell: the fallen angels, people from other religious faiths, those who persistently choose to oppose God, and those who die removed from love. But then, although she again affirms her commitment to the church's teachings (remember, people who opposed the church in Julian's day often got burned at the stake!), she hears Christ say: "That which is impossible for you is not impossible for Me. I will keep My word in all things, and I will make absolutely everything well." She goes on to say: "And so I learned to believe these two seemingly contradictory truths, holding them both in my mind at the same time. I resolved to continue within the Church's teachings while I also believed that in the end, absolutely everything will be well, just as our Protector had showed me."

Meditation 36

Martin Schleske, *The Sound of Life's Unspeakable Beauty*, translated by Janet Gesme (Grand Rapids: Eerdmans, 2020).

Meditation 42

On nonviolent resistance, of course, dwell in Martin Luther King Jr.'s writings. From my own chosen tradition, read the Mennonite peacemaker John Paul Lederach. Nonviolence International and Community Peacemaker Teams also do beautiful work. If you're interested in outcome-based research on nonviolent movements, see Erica Chenoweth and Maria J. Stephan, *Why Civil Resistance Works: The Strategic Logic of Nonviolent Conflict* (New York: Columbia University Press, 2019).

BOTANICAL
NOTES

⸺

The art in *Dearworthy* was all created digitally via sketching/painting rather than simply manipulating existing images. Reference photos were mostly my own, but I also consulted online images, the app PictureThis, and Allen J. Coombes, *The Book of Leaves: A Leaf-by-Leaf Guide to Six Hundred of the World's Great Trees*, edited by Zsolt Debreczy (Chicago: University of Chicago Press, 2010). I am also indebted to my dear friend Catherine Miller Harper, naturalist and science educator, who supplied stunning photos of white water rose and nodding thistle head.

You will see that I encountered a good number of these plants at Churchill Park in Glen Ellyn, Illinois. This may suggest that I live there, but I do not; a good friend hosted me in Glen Ellyn for several months during the first year of the COVID-19 pandemic, while my newly purchased condo in Chicago was being rehabbed. All these plants remind me of Cindy and Dan's kindness.

Meditation 1: This is the only image I drew without reference to a specific plant. During my neighborhood walks, I often pick up branches that Chicago's winds have blown down. They make great kindling for my firepit.

Meditation 2: I went looking for a heart-shaped leaf and found images from the foxglove tree (*Paulownia tomentosa*), which is native to China, Japan, and other East Asian countries.

Meditation 3: My friend Darrell gave me a raspberry plant (*Rubus idaeus*), and I tried to keep it alive in a large pot in my garden area. Alas, it did not survive, but while it was alive, I was enchanted by its compound leaves with their three leaflets.

Meditation 4: Wanting to represent Julian's home region, I learned that the English oak (*Quercus robur*), also called pedunculate oak, is the most common tree in Norwich and the county of Norfolk and is also found across most of Europe and Russia. These trees can live a thousand years or longer. Each tree sends down a deep taproot and then lateral roots, which can spread up to ninety feet from the trunk.

Meditation 5: The flowering dogwood (*Cornus florida*), a small North American tree, thrives in my neighborhood, though it's not common here. When my father died, my stepmother planted a dogwood in his memory on the grounds of the church they attended in Siloam Springs, Arkansas.

Meditation 6: The peacock plant (*Goeppertia makoyana*) is native to Brazil, but I encountered it at the Lincoln Park Conservatory in Chicago. The leaves do not grow in this butterfly-like configuration; I drew one spectacular leaf and then reproduced it in this pattern to represent how I might, in my human ignorance, try to create a world that is flawless, symmetrical, free of sin.

Meditation 7: The bald cypress (*Taxodium distichum*) is a North American native. I was struck by its beautiful peeling bark when I encountered it at Churchill Park in Glen Ellyn, Illinois.

Meditation 8: Aren't hazelnuts beautiful? In the UK, they're often referred to as *cobnuts*; in Europe, they're also known as *filberts* (probably in honor of Saint Philbert, whose feast day is August 20, a date when hazelnuts begin to ripen); and in Gaelic, their name is *coll*. Their scientific name is *Corylus avellana*. Julian would have known them as *hasel-nuts*.

Meditation 9: Leaves of *Corylus avellana* around the hazelnut. Given Julian's love of fabric and clothing imagery, I drew them to suggest appliqué with stitching.

Meditation 10: The white mulberry (*Morus australis*) is native to northern China but has become quite common in the United States; this was one of several in my neighborhood. If I walk under a mulberry with ripe fruit, I always pull off one or two to eat—but I felt these early-spring branches exuded an almost unbearable vulnerability.

Meditation 11: The monkey mask monstera (*Monstera deliciosa*), also known as Swiss cheese plant, is native to southern Mexico and Central America and has become quite common as a houseplant in North America and other temperate zones.

Meditation 12: Bitternut hickory (*Carya cordiformis*) is native to the eastern and midwestern United States. Its leaves are compound with a symmetrical arrangement of (usually) seven leaflets.

Meditation 13: The fragrant plantain lily, or August lily (*Hosta plantaginea*), grows in the courtyard of the building where I live, though its origins are in China. It blooms briefly but stunningly, with brilliant white lily-shaped blossoms.

Meditation 14: This particular white water rose (*Nymphaea alba*) was not just white but had streaks of magenta, dazzling with its center of intense yellow stamens. It's a kind of water lily that's native to Europe, Asia, and parts of North Africa.

Meditation 15: When I was five years old, I was transfixed by a little clump of violets in the yard of our home in Overland Park, Kansas. They were so beautiful, I couldn't believe they were wild. When I discovered common meadow violets (*Viola sororia*) in the yard outside my Chicago condo, it felt like receiving a blessing on my new home. They are native to North America.

Meditation 16: I became acquainted with the tulip poplar or tulip tree (*Liriodendron tulipifera*) at a church picnic at Rock Cut State Park. It's actually a species of magnolia that has striking cup-shaped flowers and is native to eastern North America. My attention was caught by its leaf, with the center vein ending not in a point but an indentation, like hair parted in the middle.

Meditation 17: These silver maple (*Acer saccharinum*) pods blow into my garden every May and June. They are streaked with red and green when they first fall, before they dry out. I clear them out as quickly as I can to prevent seedlings from taking root among the prairie plants I'm trying to establish. But visually, they are charming!

Meditation 18: I'm familiar with guava (*guayaba* in Spanish; *Psidium guajava*) from my years in Colombia. It's native to Central and South America and the Caribbean. Guava paste from the fruit is used to make sweets, which for some reason repelled me as a teen (I enjoy the flavor now). But I had never looked closely at the leaves until I hunted down images and began to draw them. They have a lot of presence, being sturdy with thick symmetrical veins.

Meditation 19: I love drawing succulents, and this one charmed me with both its form and its name, mother of thousands (*Kalanchoe daigremontiana*, native to Madagascar). The little corms along its edges eventually fall into the ground and quickly take root and germinate.

Meditation 20: The kingcup or claret cup cactus (*Echinocereus triglochidiatus*) is native to northern Mexico and the southwestern United States. If you're not familiar with it, search for images online or visit a garden shop; I wish I could have rendered the brilliant red of its bloom for this book.

Meditation 21: Palm Sunday is one of my favorite holy days, and palm branches with their smiling shape seem so appropriate to accompany Julian's laughter. These are from the Canary Island date palm (*Phoenix canariensis*).

Meditation 22: I wanted to capture the movement of weeping willow (*Salix babylonica*) branches in the slightest breeze. I love standing in the magical little "room" under a willow with its moving walls of stem and leaf. This tree is native to China, but variants of it are now planted widely across the United States.

Meditation 23: I met this compass plant (also called cup plant; *Silphium perfoliatum*) at Churchill Park in Glen Ellyn, Illinois. It's native to the eastern and central United States, and it grows up to eight feet and blooms bright yellow in summer, looking a lot like a sunflower. Its lower leaves orient themselves north-south to minimize exposure to the intense sunlight of deep summer.

Meditation 24: I love the form of northern mountain ash leaves; to me, it suggests the unity and distinctions within the Godhead. Botanists treat each set of these leaflets as one whole leaf rather than a stem with fifteen separate leaves. The shrub grows throughout New England, eastern Canada, and southern Greenland.

Meditation 25: I met a northern white cedar (*Thuja occidentalis*) in the Glen Ellyn, Illinois, garden of friends; it's native to the northeastern United States and eastern Canada. My friends cultivated several of these cedars as a row of shrubs, but the plant can grow as high as eighty feet. I loved the way that my drawing quickly began to resemble embroidery, which seems so appropriate to Julian's imagery.

Meditation 26: Eastern bottlebrush grass (*Elymus hystrix*) is another native plant that grows in Churchill Park, Glen Ellyn, Illinois.

Meditation 27: Ferns are my favorite plants. I encountered this one when hiking at Matthiessen State Park in central Illinois. It's called Christmas fern (*Polystichum acrostichoides*); I love the variegations on its fronds.

Meditation 28: From the start, wild strawberries (*Fragaria virginiana*), North American natives, took root happily in my little prairie garden and are creating a lovely ground cover. They send out red runners and bear tiny sour, bright-red berries.

Meditation 29: In the fall, a tree near my home bears an abundance of serviceberries (*Amelanchier* genus; I could not determine the particular species), and it was a joy to draw this one laden branch.

Meditation 30: After my family moved to Colombia, I grew up around banana trees, which have a succulent rather than woody trunk, so they are not really trees; cultivated bananas are either *Musa acuminata* or *Musa balbisiana*. The leaves are used as umbrellas, to wrap packages, to thatch roofs, or (cut up) to steam tamales.

Meditation 31: This nodding thistle (*Carduus nutans*) is about to bloom into a rose or magenta head composed of hundreds of tiny individual flowers. Unfortunately, these plants, native to Eurasia, are invasive in the U.S. Midwest.

Meditation 32: I pulled a leaf off a neighborhood mulberry tree (*Morus australis*; not the same one as in meditation 10) and was charmed by the difference between top (darker) and bottom (lighter).

Meditation 33: Purplestem angelica (*Angelica atropurpurea*) is native to eastern North America. The one I encountered at Churchill Park in Glen Ellyn, Illinois, was a bit past its blossoming prime. This plant lives for several years but blossoms just once—gloriously!—during that time.

Meditation 34: The blue grama grass (*Bouteloua gracilis*) I came across must have been under drought stress; the plant's head is usually curved just slightly, not circling back to the stem like this. This grass is native to central North America.

Meditation 35: These papaya (*Carica papaya*) leaves remind me of a delightful hour I spent with friends exploring the grounds of the former home of a Swiss mint farmer in San Francisco, Putumayo, Colombia. Isn't that an unexpected set of circumstances! I encountered the plant near the ground but already with very large leaves, as is typical of papayas, but I didn't recognize it at the time since it hadn't grown yet into a tree. It's native to southern Mexico and Central America, but today it's cultivated much more widely throughout tropical regions.

Meditation 36: Blue echeveria (*Echeveria secunda*) grows in the lush garden of my childhood friend Dorys Arias outside Pitalito, Huila, Colombia. Its succulent leaves really do have a blue tint. Many butterflies depend on this plant, which is native to Central and South America.

BOTANICAL NOTES

Meditation 37: This image is based on a more extensive drawing that's been circulating for decades of the root systems of many Illinois native prairie plants. The deep roots help these plants to survive wildfires and controlled burns. Included here are (left to right) switchgrass, white wild indigo, little bluestem, rosinweed, purple prairie clover, June grass, cylindric blazing star, buffalo grass.

Meditation 38: With these leaves and acorns, we are back again to the English or pedunculate oak (*Quercus robur*).

Meditation 39: This stem of Eastern redbud (*Cercis canadensis*), native to eastern and central North America, had visibly aging leaves at its tip, while younger leaves were growing nearer the trunk. It seemed an excellent image to represent our connectedness to one another.

Meditation 40: Catalina ironwood (*Lyonothamnus floribundus*) is a tree native to California's Channel Islands. I love the distinctive pattern of its evergreen leaves.

Meditation 41: Daylilies (*Hemerocallis fulva*) in permutations of orange, yellow, and red bring much cheer to the streets of my neighborhood in the summer. I picture them trumpeting the Great Deed at the end of time.

Meditation 42: I was astonished by the dense, intricate inner petals of this hybrid tea rose (*Rosa hybrida*) growing in my sister's Southern California garden.

Meditation 43: On a rainforest trek while I accompanied the Afro-Colombian Cacarica community in Chocó, northwestern Colombia, we came upon this gorgeous shining bird of paradise (*Heliconia metallica*) standing taller than me on its muscular succulent stem. Wild, compelling beauty like this helps me believe that indeed all shall be well.

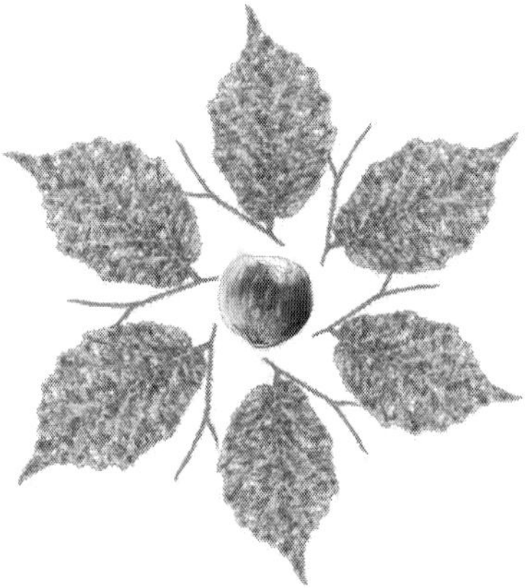

All Shall Be Well

A Modern-Language Version of the Revelation of Julian Norwich

The great spiritual classic by Julian of Norwich is now available in modern, easy-to-comprehend language that stays true to Julian's original meanings. Her ancient wisdom is as relevant now as it was in the 14th century's world of plague, prejudice, and war. Discover Julian's joyous affirmation of the certainty of Divine love, a love that overcomes all.

"Julian would be pleased with this rendering of the Showings into contemporary English. The even-handed blending here of simple language and the grandeur of Julian's content is flawless; and the happy result is that the Showings slip into our minds and hearts as effortlessly as if the mystic of Norwich were speaking to us herself, face-to-face and soul-to-soul."

– Phyllis Tickle

Hazelnuts from Julian of Norwich
Meditations on Divine Love

"The Spirit showed me a tiny thing, the size of a hazelnut," wrote the fourteenth-century mystic, Julian of Norwich. In Julian's vision, the fragile and insignificant hazelnut contains all of Creation—and yet it endures "because God loves it."

Seven hundred years before Rob Bell wrote *Love Wins*, Julian had already offered the world a vision of God's all-encompassing love. These prayer-poems, based on *All Shall Be Well: A Modern-Language Version of the Revelation of Julian Norwich*, are an accessible introduction to Julian's joyous theology of love.

"Take this book from my heart to yours," she wrote. "If you forget all the rest, remember this: Love is everything. Love is God."

The Cookbook of Julian of Norwich
From Hazelnuts to Pottages
A Collection of Medieval Recipes

Accompanied by inspiration from *All Shall Be Well: A Modern-Language Version of the Showings of Julian of Norwich.*

Julian of Norwich was deeply concerned with the spiritual world—but she believed it was firmly rooted in the practical ordinary details of daily life, including eating and tasting. Her thoughts pair well with the recipes of her day, for she writes again and again of the nourishment God gives to us and the sweet taste of the Divine.

Joy and love are the two words that best sum up Julian's spirituality. May this cookbook, based on the food of Julian's lifetime as well as her writing, give you joy... and the certainty that you are Divinely loved.

Sacred Soil
A Gardener's Book of Reflection

In these fifteen intimate essays, Melina Rudman explores the pain of loss and the joy of connection, all within the context of her garden. She writes of gardening as a spiritual practice, one that has the power to ground us in the seasons and cycles of Nature. Gardening, she says, plants us firmly in the circle of birth, life, and death, "smack dab in the middle of life's gore and glory." While gardening focuses on the world of touch and sight and scent, it also opens doors to deeper realities. It teaches us resilience; it shows us how to let go; it comforts our aching hearts; it leads us to repentance—and it offers us a conduit to the Divine.

Spirit, I give thanks
that I am held in a great
web of Being,
where the energy of earth
and memory,
tree and thought, flower
and emotion,
are all knit together
into You.

The Greening
Garden Thoughts with Celtic Prayers

This little book contains "green thoughts" from writers who gardened across the centuries, thoughts that speak about the beauty and meaning of gardens. These words are combined with the author's personal prayers, based on the ancient Celtic words from the Carmina Gadelica. Whether you garden yourself or only enjoy looking at gardens, this collection of thoughts will remind you of the deep connection with the life force that sustains not only every green thing but also our own lives and the entire cosmos.

*Here in my garden,
I bend my knee
to the beauty I see
beneath me,
to the beauty I see above me,
to the beauty
I see all around me.
O Great Being,
Spirit of Beauty,
bestow on me eyes to see
beauty in leaf,
beauty in flower,
beauty in love,
beauty in power,
beauty in stem,
beauty in fruit,
beauty in soil,
beauty in root.*

Anamchara
Books

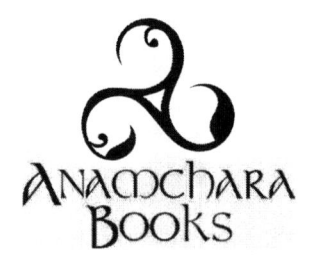

AnamcharaBooks.com

Made in the USA
Middletown, DE
19 February 2025